The Responsible Church

The Responsible Church

Edited by Edwin Barker

Secretary of the Board for Social Responsibility
of the Church Assembly

London S·P·C·K 1966

First published in 1966
by S.P.C.K.
Holy Trinity Church
Marylebone Road
London N.W.1

Printed in Great Britain by
Billing and Sons Ltd
Guildford and London

Contents

1. THE NATURE OF CHRISTIAN
   INVOLVEMENT IN SOCIETY   1
   by R. R. Williams

2. THE WELFARE SOCIETY   14
   by Nesta Roberts

3. THE IMPACT OF TECHNOLOGY   21
   by D. G. Christopherson

4. RACE, CULTURE, NATIONALISM   40
   by Philip Mason

5. OVERSEAS AID AND
   CHRISTIAN RESPONSIBILITY   53
   by James Mark

6. DEFENCE AND DISARMAMENT   62
   by Anthony Buzzard

7. MAN'S DOMINION   77
   by Hugh Montefiore

The Contributors to this Volume

The Right Reverend R. R. WILLIAMS is Bishop of Leicester.

NESTA ROBERTS is a journalist and is Health Correspondent of *The Guardian*.

Dr D. G. CHRISTOPHERSON, O.B.E., F.R.S., is Vice-Chancellor and Warden of the University of Durham. He was formerly Professor of Mechanical Engineering at Leeds University, and Professor of Applied Science at Imperial College, London.

PHILIP MASON is Director of the Institute of Race Relations.

JAMES MARK is a civil servant, at present with the Ministry of Overseas Development; he is a member of the Christian Frontier Council and is the author of a number of articles on contemporary theology and of *The Question of Christian Stewardship*.

Rear Admiral Sir ANTHONY BUZZARD, Bt., C.B., D.S.O., O.B.E., retired from the Royal Navy in 1954 as Director of Naval Intelligence, is now Armament Director in Vickers Ltd; he is a founder member of the Institute for Strategic Studies and has served on various British and World Councils of Churches Commissions on war in the nuclear age.

Canon HUGH MONTEFIORE is Vicar of Great St Mary's, Cambridge, and Canon Theologian of Coventry Cathedral. He was formerly Dean of Gonville and Caius College and a University Lecturer in New Testament.

1 The Nature of
Christian Involvement
in Society

R. R. Williams

This book is intended to deepen, strengthen, and extend social responsibility in the Church. It is meant to assist the individual Christian in his duty of being socially responsible; it is meant to assist individual local Churches to be socially responsible; it is meant to help "the Church" (and in the first place the Church of England) to fulfil its social responsibilities.

What is social responsibility? It is not an alternative to individual, personal, or spiritual responsibility, although the acceptance or rejection of social responsibility may be a decisive factor in spiritual progress or spiritual regression. It is not a substitute for moral responsibility in the sense that being socially responsible makes up for being irresponsible in the more conventional realms of moral decision. It is, however, something distinctive—it is responsibility directed towards the whole fabric of society, responsibility for the way society is organized, for the values which it elects to respect and treasure, or alternatively to despise and reject. Of course in a democracy the ultimate *legal* responsibility for society lies with Parliament, or whatever organ the population has chosen as the expression of its will and purpose. But the existence of Parliament or its equivalent does not remove from the individual citizen his responsibility both to watch and in his measure influence Parliament, and also to comport himself in all those relationships which are not governed by Parliament in such a way as to be socially responsible. To be socially responsible is to use one's life and influence so

1

that the good of the whole society is benefited. Sometimes big national issues are involved, sometimes quite small personal neighbourhood problems. To be socially responsible is to consider at all times the good of the whole, while not seeking to escape from those direct responsibilities which weigh immediately upon fathers, mothers, husbands, wives, children, neighbours, employers, employed, shopkeepers, customers, and all the other categories of "mutual responsibility and interdependence".

The responsibility of "the Church" within any one sovereign State is twofold. It is first to exercise upon government at all levels—central and local—such influence as it can in order to bring society more closely in line with what it discerns to be God's will for society at any one period of history and in any one part of the world. It will do this by all the means in its power. In England there are the bishops' benches in the House of Lords from which comment can be and is made on social and political issues from day to day. There are resolutions passed by official Church assemblies and publicized in the press. There are correspondence columns in daily newspapers and opportunities on radio and television. But in addition to all this exercise of public influence there is social responsibility of quite another kind, namely that which has as its aim the education and inspiration of the Church's own members in the right attitude to adopt in current problems, and in that spirit of neighbourly service for which government action can never be a wholly satisfactory substitute. Direct "philanthropic" service (to use an outmoded but strictly relevant adjective) comes in here, and this branch of social responsibility is the *raison d'être* of the Church's mother and baby homes, adoption societies, children's homes and orphanages, and so on.

All this has been described as coming within social responsibility in one sovereign State. Many problems now confronting mankind cannot be so confined—they concern relations between States, and relations between groups situated in different States. Modern life is a life of complex international relationships, of the migration of peoples, of the interchange of trade, of the fear of war. In some of these situations "the Church" in one nation, or many nations, can make a direct contribution (for example, through Oxfam or Inter-Church Aid); while in others it can contribute only as it can influence its own government to adopt certain policies rather than others.

Nor must we suggest that in these situations the Church knows all the answers. In the past "the Church" as an organized institution has sometimes been right and sometimes been wrong, and this will doubtless be the case again. The light thrown by history is, as Coleridge said, a light thrown on the waves only from the *stern* of mankind's boat —we can see backward, but hardly at all forward. It is the Church's task not only to be responsible, but to be responsive, to be alert to new issues, to new revelations of God's purpose for mankind, some of which will appear not from ecclesiastical sources at all, but from developments appearing to be entirely secular. Only as "Church" it will look at all things in the light of that movement in human thought and experience which it believes to have come, and to be coming from God in Christ, a movement of which the Old Testament records the preparation, the Gospels the climax, the Epistles, and all subsequent Church history the subsequent, uneven but still unmistakable development.

It may be helpful at this point to survey briefly the emergence of "social responsibility" as a theme in the Bible, beginning with the Old Testament. It must be realized that the whole of the Old Testament literature was produced within and for a very confined community, the Hebrew people, located for most of the relevant period in a very small part of Southern Palestine, centred in the City of Jerusalem. Some of the material of course arose within the Northern Kingdom of Israel, with headquarters at Samaria, some was written in exile or in the Diaspora. Nevertheless, the political entities involved were relatively insignificant. It is a miracle that so much of such great value has survived.

The Book Deuteronomy (probably dating from the time of Josiah, King of Judah, 639–608 B.C.) reveals a remarkable development of social responsibility. It must be taken as representing the views of the prophetic school, and although all is put into the mouth of Moses, it conveys the prophetic idea of what God required in the social life of the agrarian communities of Judah in the seventh century. In another book[1] I have summarized the message of this very wonderful treatise, and I repeat this summary here.

Here the first and dominant message is the importance of loving and worshipping Jahveh, the God to whom Israel owed its deliverance, and of worshipping in that place where it should please Him to set His Name, viz. Jerusalem. But alongside this there is a corollary. It was because of God's goodness and mercy that He had deigned to choose Israel, and to deliver them, and this was part of His essential character and Being. The same Lord, who "had a delight in [Israel's] fathers to love them", a "God of gods and Lord of Lords, a mighty and a terrible, which regardeth not persons, nor taketh reward", was a God who "doth execute the judgment of the fatherless and widow, and loveth the stranger, in giving him food and raiment" (Deut. 10. 15–18). The commandment quickly follows (v. 19) "Love ye therefore the stranger; for ye were strangers in the land of Egypt." From this principle follow the many injunctions of the book concerning the treatment of the poor and destitute. The year of release of debt, for instance, is to be rigidly enforced, and the needy borrower is not to be refused because that year is nigh at hand (Deut. 15. 7–10). Justice is to be done, and difficult disputes are to be brought to "the priests the Levites, and unto the judge" (Deut. 17. 9). Cities of refuge are to be provided for innocent victims of capital charges (Deut. 19. 4 ff). Members of the army who have particular reasons for avoiding the dangers of battle—new houses, or new wives—are to be sent home on compassionate grounds (Deut. 20. 5–9). Valuable trees are not to be cut down unnecessarily in military operations (Deut. 20. 20). All kinds of social rules and conventions are laid down, some of them very curious, but mostly inspired by a spirit of kindness and consideration for the helpless. It is thus a duty—not a voluntary matter—to assist "a brother's ox or ass" if he falls by the way. If sexual relations were forced upon an engaged girl by another man she was not to be blamed, but the man

[1] *The Bible in Worship and Ministry* (Mowbray, 1962, now o.p.).

must die (Deut. 22. 25 ff). If an unbetrothed virgin were seduced, the marriage must be completed (Deut. 22. 28 ff). Usury to fellow-Israelites was forbidden (Deut. 23. 19). Cornfields were not to be reaped to the last ear, but something was to be left for the poor gleaner (Deut. 24. 18). There were even some simple town-planning rules, particularly concerning the safety of houses. "When thou buildest a new house, then thou shalt make a battlement for thy roof, that thou bring not blood upon thy house, if any man fall from thence" (Deut. 22. 8). These are only examples of the ethical standards which were favoured in the early prophetic school which produced Deuteronomy. Its subsequent canonization, and the prominence given to Deuteronomic passages in the Shema, show that they entered into the classical ethical tradition of the Hebrew people.

The eighth and seventh-century prophets, both in Israel and Judah, devoted much of their speaking (and writing if they wrote at all) to the theme of social justice. "Establish judgment in the gate", says Amos (5. 15) and this could serve as a heading for much of what they said. Israel was continually urged to put its hope not in purely religious or cultic observances, but in giving justice to the poor, in caring for the fatherless and the widow, in resisting oppression. Amos extends his challenge to surrounding nations, and arraigns not only Judah and Israel but Syria, Moab, and other lands. Here was a foretaste of the "International Departments" which now exist alongside "Social Departments" in many Churches.

The important point to note in all this is that God was using his prophets to unveil new needs, new responsibilities to his people. It is only in looking back that we can see the emerging pattern. At the time only "prophets" could see it —that is why many of them were persecuted and even killed. But looking back we can see that God was at work. He was, so to speak, revealing his character by the impact of his prophets upon history. To be frank, we should have, could have, no picture of God's *character*, as contrasted with his "eternal power and divinity", except through those who have seen the *social* demands on God's people as expressions of the voice and mind of God. That is why from very early times man was called on not only to love God, but to love his neighbour as himself. It was only our Lord who brought these two commandments into direct and similar (if not equal) status, but the two orders had stood there on the pages of Scripture from time immemorial.

It was when tender hearts had seen the needs of the fatherless and widows that men came to see that God is "a father of the fatherless and defendeth the cause of the widows" (Ps. 68. 5, Prayer Book Version). True, the psalmists and prophets linked this "character" of God with his adoption of the "fatherless" Israel and his espousal of the widowed (exiled) nation, but the first awakening to this "social responsibility" on God's part must have come through the compassionate response of those who had eyes to see the plight of the destitute, and ears to hear the cry of the oppressed.

How does the life and mission of our Lord fit into this pattern? The Incarnation is so infinitely far-reaching in its significance that any attempt to press it into some preconceived mould must be dangerous. On the other hand, if Christ is the True Light, the light that he sheds must ultimately blend with, and not clash against, all other true light on man's needs and destinies. I think we shall see that the life and teaching of Jesus *does* irradiate further the line of thought we have been following, namely the idea that God is always showing men new areas of need, new calls to *sensitivity*, and no one did this more conspicuously than Jesus himself.

His message was, primarily, the immediacy and presence of God's rule, which was made real in and around himself, and conveyed into the lives of men by the message of the Gospel and the miracles of healing. The first charge given to the apostles was certainly "supernatural" in its power, but it was very earthly in its application. See, for example, Matt. 10. 7, 8: "The kingdom of heaven is at hand. Heal the sick, raise the dead, cleanse the lepers, cast out devils." Heaven's rule meant earth's deliverance. Further, our Lord was clearly both loved (and hated) for his new approach to "sinners". If one thing stands out in the Gospels more than another, it is that Jesus rejected the conventional separation of his countrymen into "righteous" and "sinners" and opened his own heart and company to the latter. "This man receiveth sinners and eateth with them", was the charge made against him. The contacts with Matthew the tax-gatherer, Mary Magdalene, the woman in Luke 7, Zacchaeus at Jericho, all point in the same direction, as do the parables of the lost sheep, the lost coin, and the lost son in Luke 15. Christ was "an accepting Christ", one who believed it to be his Father's will that (unlike the elder son in the story of the Prodigal) he should welcome to love, understanding, and forgiveness those who had not kept the law and hence were regarded as outcasts.

When it was said later that "Christ died for the ungodly" (Rom. 5. 6) it was not merely a statement that in some mysterious way Christ's Cross had an atoning power. It probably means that in a literal sense Christ had died as the price he had to pay for his friendship with sinners.

All this means that through the words and works of Christ a new phase of social responsibility had been opened up in the world, a phase where men's deserts had ceased to be the final word, but where a Love had been glimpsed capable of absorbing, neutralizing, cleansing, and redeeming the worst of men and the worst in men. This is what St Paul meant when he said that Christ was made sin for us, that we might be made the righteousness of God in him.

Already we are advancing to the "post-Resurrection" impact of our Lord and his work.

It cannot be said that on any superficial view the Epistles (or the apostolic age) made a very direct contribution to the development of Christian social responsibility. The circum-stances in which the Church was placed virtually made this impossible. The Christians were a tiny minority in a world of Jewish piety and Gentile power. Their situation was akin to that of Christians in certain Asiatic countries, although in some of these, historic connections with Western powers have made social contributions possible even after the arrival of political independence. What is true is that the Epistles represent the glowing core of ardent Christian faith from which all future generations of Christians were to be kindled with the ardour of Divine Love. This 1 Cor. 13, in its context but an exposition of "the best gift" of the Spirit, became for all future Christians the classic expression of what true selfless charity could mean. 1 John 4 showed the ideal of that love which was to unite Christians, the inevitable result of a true appreciation of the love "which the Father has bestowed upon us". Gal. 5 showed that the characteristic gifts of the Spirit were love, joy, and peace, a trio of virtues followed by six other characteristics, largely social in character. It was to be the task of successive generations to discuss endlessly new applications of an attitude to life which owed everything to Christ and his first apostles. Not least could be mentioned the inherited thought that God's purpose was to sum up all things in Christ, a Pauline expression for the Johannine vision of Christ as the Logos, or Word of God, the ultimate Mind behind, in, and through all created things and the whole created universe. It is this thought that enables Christians, without disloyalty to "the truth as it is in Jesus" to see in all scientific discovery, and in all technological achievement profitable to human health and happiness, further manifestations of the glory of the Eternal Word.

There is of course one expression of social responsibility to be found in the Epistles and that is the collection organized by St Paul in the Gentile Churches on behalf of "the poor saints" at Jerusalem. I have often been tempted to inquire whether these "poor saints" could possibly have been ordinary Jewish people, not necessarily Christians. I am afraid the balance of the argument is decisively in favour of the "saints" being impoverished Christians, but even so the story is a real example of social responsibility, in this case we might say of "inter-Church aid". I imagine that in the early days Jerusalem was the only centre where there were enough Christian poor to constitute a problem, and of course to St Paul this collection became a sacrament of Jewish-Gentile unity. It is interesting that in some of the latest books of the New Testament we find references to a group, almost an order, of widows (see 1 Tim. 5. 3–16). This suggests that as the Christian community grew in the Gentile cities such as Antioch and Ephesus, the needs of the Christian poor once more began to take on "social" proportions. Widows in local Churches had of course been cared for since the earliest days (see Acts 6. 1).

It is now necessary to take a flying trip through the Christian centuries and to note how at different times the social conscience of the Church has been stirred into action by new insights that have come to God's people, mostly through the eyes of specially gifted prophetic souls.

The first stopping point might be the "conversion" of Constantine in A.D. 312. Although Constantine was not baptized till about A.D. 337, he administered his Empire with many Christian standards in mind. "Social responsibility" at that time could be expressed only by an autocratic Emperor, and the remarkable thing is how soon the Christian leaven began to leaven the very large pagan lump. Constantine began to humanize the criminal law and to mitigate the conditions of slavery. By making grants to support poor children he discouraged the exposure of unwanted babies. He made Sunday a public holiday. This was just a first example of how society itself could be changed under the influence of Christian ideas. It is not to suggest that Constantine was a mature or intelligent Christian!

St Augustine represents another landmark in this matter, although rather an ambiguous one. In his great work *The City of God* he grapples with the immense problem of the downfall of the Roman Empire. As a Platonist, he often seems to say that the kingdom of this world is evil and temporary, only to be contrasted adversely with the kingdom which is eternal in the heavens. But he *has* to consider the question of the purpose of the earthly State. He usually states that its only purpose is a temporary, remedial one— that of containing evil within bounds. But even when he is criticizing the evils of earthly kingdoms, he is automatically suggesting that they *might* pursue better, more godly ends. In this way he prepared for the teaching of St Thomas

Aquinas, who eight hundred years later was to pick up the teaching of Aristotle, admit that man was at least in part a political animal, and that the erection of Christian States was among the highest of human achievements.

The work of St Thomas Aquinas is important in a number of ways. For one thing he is a Christian thinker who thinks positively about the ordering of the State. As the States of "Christendom" took shape, this was of immense importance. Democracy in our sense of the word was unknown and unthinkable, and the whole question was what principles were to govern those who governed, whether they were kings or popes. St Thomas had a positive view of authority. He saw that the universe was governed by one God, and deduced from this that government in a kingdom by one man was the best. We now know all the limitations of autocracy, but in that time it was vital to establish the principle that the king's rule was exercised within the framework of God's rule, that the king's laws were subject to God's laws. This was social responsibility, relevant to the times. It is a mistake to think (as the late Canon S. G. Evans sometimes seemed to do in *The Social Hope of the Christian Church*) that Christian insights are only those which inspire the revolutionary, anarchic elements in society. God is a God of order and not of confusion, and in certain situations a strong hierarchical form of government may represent the best chance for the common man to live his life in peace and relative prosperity. Equally, when the State can be so ordered that "Everyman" can play his part in the determination of its policy, any system that provides less than this falls under judgement. The first book of Hooker's, *Ecclesiastical Policy*, incorporates Aquinas' theory of law, and mediates it into the Anglican tradition.

As an example of how very modern were some of the insights of St Thomas, let me quote a passage from his work, "On Princely Government", in which he shows an example of medieval "town and country planning".

One who is about to establish a city or a realm must, in the first place, choose a suitable site; healthy, to ensure the health of the inhabitants; fertile, to provide for their sustenance; one which will delight the eye with its loveliness and give natural security against hostile attack . . . Having chosen the site, the next task . . . is to plan the area to meet all the requirements of a civic life . . . One must decide where to build the towns and where to leave the countryside open . . . Centres of study, open places for military training, and markets all have to be taken into consideration. If it is a city . . . sites must be assigned to churches, to administrative offices, and to the workshops of various trades . . . Finally, provision must be made so that no person goes in want.[2]

Here, indeed, is social responsibility expressing itself through the author of the *Summa Theologica*, the Angelic Doctor, Thomas, Dominican of Paris.

Space fails to allow mention of all the subsequent insights that have come to Christians in almost every age. The monasteries in their heyday, provided refuge centres, medical care, and poor relief. Parliament began to care for the poor in a systematic way in the reign of the first Elizabeth, while endless merchants laid out their new wealth in grammar schools and almshouses. By 1662 the Church of England was having its first thoughts about "the natives of our plantations".[3]

All through the nineteenth century, Christians (but not only Christians) were made aware of new areas in national or overseas life where a new social challenge called for a new response in service or agitation. Slavery, the death penalty for theft, prisons and prisoners, overseas missions, factory conditions, education for all—one by one all these subjects came into the ken of sensitive and "socially responsible" souls. It is useless to condemn those who had not seen the need for reform till a Wilberforce, an Elizabeth Fry, a Shaftesbury, a Florence Nightingale, saw the need and pointed the way forward. Each generation can see only with the eyes of its prophets. The only area for blame lies where

[2] *Aquinas: Selected Political Writings*, A. P. Entrèves (Blackwell, 1948).

[3] See the Preface of the Book of Common Prayer in reference to the service for the Baptism of those of Riper Years.

B

men had been shown the need for change, and out of selfishness or inertia refused to act upon the revelations made to them.

So we come to this book, and its six chapters. Each of them opens up a subject which to the Board for Social Responsibility seems important in the current situation, and worthy of thought and study in days of "mutual responsibility and interdependence".

It is significant that only two of them deal exclusively with "home affairs"—Miss Nesta Roberts' chapter on *The Welfare Society* and Dr Christopherson's on *The Impact of Technology*. The first briefly, the second more extensively, deals with an element in our modern social life that Christians may easily ignore, or even fight against, in the belief that it is harmful to the work and witness of the Church, and hostile to the kind of society to which Christians have been accustomed or for which they have hoped. Neither I nor the Board would feel ourselves bound by every sentence of our Contributors, but we believe they are looking in the right direction. We think that the areas covered by these two writers are areas in which the Church is being called to a new sensitivity, a new awareness of God's unfolding purpose in Christ.

The articles by Philip Mason on *Race, Culture, Nationalism*, by James Mark on *Overseas Aid and Christian Responsibility*, and on *Defence and Disarmament* by Admiral Sir Anthony Buzzard, all deal with problems that are basically international, although each sovereign nation, including our own, has to come to terms with them in one way or another. Finally in *Man's Dominion*, Canon Hugh Montefiore presents us with an apocalypse, an unveiling of things that are coming to pass on the earth almost without our knowing, yet which are going to affect the lives of generations yet unborn in every part of the globe. Here, indeed, is a prophetic word, compelling us to say, not "Am I my brother's keeper?", but "Am I my grandchild's keeper, or the keeper of my great-great grandchild?" I will not spoil the reader's pleasure, or blunt the challenge which lies before him by anticipating what is in this book. I will only thank those who have contributed, and include in my thanks Mr Edwin Barker, who planned and edited the whole volume. And I commend the book to Christian readers, for their earnest and prayerful consideration.

2 The Welfare Society

Nesta Roberts

There is a prayer which, with minor variations, is common to a large number of schools and colleges. It asks, in effect, that the Lord shall bless and prosper the foundation, in order that it may continue to produce just persons to serve God in Church and State. At the time when most of those prayers were framed, serving God in Church and State was usually interpreted as entering Holy Orders or doing one's duty in the rather narrowly restricted field which was then considered suitable for an educated man, as a Member of Parliament, or magistrate, or officer of the armed Forces, as a lawyer, or doctor, or schoolmaster. To-day it is probably true to say that, while our conception of serving God in the Church has broadened to include laity as well as clergy, our concept of serving God in the State has dwindled and been impoverished. True, the sphere of activity considered proper for an educated man or woman has been greatly extended, but the number of educated men and women, even when they are practising Christians, who consciously set out to be civil servants, or university lecturers, or postmen, or publicans, or actuaries, to the greater glory of God cannot, one feels, be large.

If, instead of "the State", one refers specifically to "the Welfare State", the reaction sometimes provoked suggests not simply that the Welfare State is regarded as godless, but that it, and so, by extension, all who are employed in its social services, are seen as opposed, if not overtly hostile, to the Church and all its works.

Why? For what reason do the members of the Body of Christ which, for 2000 years, has felt it had a duty to minister to the material as well as the spiritual needs of his children,

14

feel resentful instead of triumphant at having worked themselves out of the more obvious aspects of their job? How can
they fail to see that the Welfare State is love in action,
founded on the Christian compassion that feels the care of
the old and the young and the orphaned, the sick and the
handicapped and the helpless, to be a tender charge on the
rest of us? The profoundly Christian decision that they must
be looked after was taken in our name. Christians should be
the spearhead of the Welfare State. It is unfortunate that
history and human vanity should sometimes have combined
to make them a lagging and destructively critical rearguard.
Looking back, it is difficult to think of any form of charitable
work, using the terms in its broadest sense, whose origins did
not spring from the Church, using that word, too, in its
broad sense of the Christian community. Teaching, nursing,
rescuing the destitute, succouring the orphaned, and giving
refuge to the old, in all these the Church pointed the way.
Indeed, it might not be too fanciful to claim that S. Vincent
de Paul's Sisters of Charity foreshadowed District Nursing,
that the medical work of SS. Cosmos and Damian was a pre-
cursor of the National Health Service, and that S. Dunstan
established something which, in principle, was very like the
Probation Service. Much of this work through the years was
well done; some, inevitably, was ill done; most was done as
well as the circumstances of the time and place allowed. In
criticizing, justly, the quality of some of the social work done
in the name of the Church, it should never be forgotten that,
generally speaking, if the Church had not done it, it would,
at that period, have been left undone, and the Church had to
work with the resources, human and material, that were
available.

The consequence is that, to-day, the Church is paying the
penalty exacted of all pioneers. The State, or the local
authority as the case may be, has followed in her steps with
more money, newer buildings, better paid and better trained
staff, so that, here and there—not, it must be stressed, by any
means everywhere and in all departments of her work—the
Church is providing a service which, materially at least, is

below what has come to be accepted as the norm. What
Church members are sometimes, understandably but unfortunately, inclined to do is to claim that the Church brings
to its social work a quality lacking in that done by statutory
agencies whose workers are "only in it for the money". The
last reproach can be quickly dealt with. Increasingly, social
workers have graduated before they begin their vocational
training. For graduates and non-graduates alike, that training is quite rigorous and demanding, presupposing reasonable mental capacity as well as personal qualities which
would be a recommendation in many jobs. In the present
state of the labour market, any man or woman so equipped
could earn as much and probably more money for far less
work in a variety of other occupations. Whether they are
employed by the State, the Church, or a voluntary society,
social workers in general choose their jobs because they offer
the best opportunities of using their gifts to serve others. The
fact that the Church and the voluntary societies are trying
to raise the salaries of their workers to the State level, and
that the same person may work for a voluntary society at one
point of his or her career, and for the Welfare State at
another, makes nonsense of the idea that the two have
different ideals and outlooks. Nor, surely, would it be main-
tained that the Church's social workers should use the
opportunity provided by contact with their clients to promul-
gate the Faith. Rice bowl Christianity has little relevance to
our age and less Scriptural warrant. It is not recorded that
the Five Thousand were required to assent to any doctrinal
statement before they were fed.

   The situation has been well explained by Penelope Hall
and Ismene Howes in their recent study of Moral Welfare
work undertaken by the Church of England *The Church in
Social Work*. They quote a local authority Children's Officer
as saying: "No social worker can make a real contribution
unless she has regard to the spiritual side. One has got to
have a faith or philosophy and it has got to come across, but
whether one works in a statutory or church setting does not
make much difference to the possibilities of bringing this

about." The authors go on: "While respecting this point of view and the conviction behind it, many moral welfare workers would, we think, consider that it leaves out of account what is, for them, the crux of the situation. What really differentiates a church worker from the individual Christian working in a secular agency, we were told, is not the way in which she handles her cases, but the spiritual and moral support she obtains from the sense that she is part of a company commissioned by the Church for a particular form of service, and this more than compensates for the higher salaries and better conditions which could be obtained by transferring to secular employment." (In passing, while this is undoubtedly true, it does not give the Church a warrant for contenting herself with lower salaries and worse conditions than are customary in secular social work.)

Several considerations are raised here, of which the most immediate is the apparent failure of the Church to give recognition and pastoral support in their professional capacity, as distinct from that which they may hope to receive as individual parishioners, to those of its members who are social workers employed by a statutory body or by a secular voluntary society. No less than that of their colleagues directly responsible to the Church, their work has a Christian foundation. Is it not time that they, too, were "commissioned by the Church for a particular form of service"—the subtle, and possibly even more demanding one of going forth to all people, not to proclaim but to demonstrate the breadth and depth of Christian compassion? The second has been touched on by Miss Hall and Miss Howes in the last chapter of their book. Given that "no social worker can make a contribution unless she (or he) has regard to the spiritual side", should not the Church consider whether it has a responsibility to set up a social work training institution comparable to its existing Teacher Training Colleges, many of whose students are destined for State schools. Its professional standards and requirements would be those of the State institutions, but it would give an extra dimension to the idea of vocation—if it failed to do so there would be no reason for its existence. And, to consider another department of education, can the Church be content to know that many of its clergy are lamentably ignorant of the provisions and working of the Welfare State and think that social work to-day still means doling out soup and blankets? Those who assume a pastoral charge should surely know where to refer for specialized help when members of the flock are in difficulties.

These issues apart, should the Church itself engage in social work in the Welfare State? Provided the qualification is "in co-operation with", or "as a supplement for", rather than "as a rival to", the Welfare State, the answer must surely be overwhelmingly yes. State provision, inevitably, must cater for broad trends and majority needs. Always there will be small groups with peculiarly difficult problems, always there will be experimental projects which promise interesting results, but which no State system can back until their worth has been proved. These, traditionally, have been tasks for voluntary agencies, and, among voluntary agencies, the Church would seem to have a particular function. Certain kinds of social work are always relatively "unpopular" (in the sense that they do not draw much financial support from the public, nor many recruits to their working force) either because the work itself is unpleasant and more than usually demanding, or because it is not likely to produce "results". Among those which spring to mind are work for alcoholics, including methylated spirit drinkers, who, in human terms, are irremediably dilapidated; long-term community support for discharged mental patients; hostels for discharged prisoners, especially those for whom another conviction will mean preventive detention. There are many more. If we are not prepared to undertake these tasks where endless work and patience bring little reward in the way of tangible results, and some of which, indeed, one might call "a mission to hopeless cases" if it were not unchristian to think in those terms, what can be expected of secular agencies?

These are matters for the Church as an institution to consider as part of its social policy. For the Church as a group of individuals gathered into local communities all over the country there is another, equally vital task. The notion that the coming of the Welfare State meant the end of voluntary effort has been long a-dying, but it seems at last to have been scotched. In its place there is growing up a realization among the professionals of the contribution which can be made by amateurs. This is noticeable at many levels. The work done by volunteers in, for example, the Citizens' Advice Bureaux, or as Marriage Guidance Counsellors (for both of which they are required to take serious training) has long been recognized. Equally, the District Nurse has wide experience of organizing informal rotas of neighbours to help to care for her solitary patients. But, to-day, psychiatrists pay tribute to the work of an organization like the Samaritans, and the Home Office acknowledges the part that voluntary workers can play in prison after-care. In every department of our social services there is an almost limitless need for helpers who can offer time, kind hearts, competent hands, and normally sensible heads. Every parish should have a task force of such people, not setting up their own organization (unless they stumble upon a need which is not being met) but offering their reliable help to the local Old People's Welfare Association, or old people's homes (and this means offering friendship to their staff as well as a hand with chores), to the Mental Welfare Officers concerned about diffident ex-patients who need friendly support if they are to get back into the main stream of social life, to the Children's Department which is seeking foster homes and adult friends for children—the list can be lengthened almost indefinitely.

Finally there is a matter which concerns the Church both as an institution and as a body of Christians: that is, to help to create a climate of opinion which favours the development of "the good society". That covers encouraging vocations for social work as well as cultivating civilized attitudes towards, say, racialism, providing an accepting community for those who are struggling to their feet after mishap, or misfortune, or misdoing, as well as leading the less enterprising of our young people to discover that bingo and doing the pools need not exhaust the recreations available to them once they are married and settled. It means, in sum, exemplifying a way of life which does not confuse virtue with self-righteousness, or charity with the condoning of wrong.

3 The Impact of Technology

D. G. Christopherson

To write about Technology at the present moment is a difficult undertaking. In every newspaper headlines about the necessity for industrial progress compete with others asserting that technical advance is always accompanied by a loss; a loss expressed not only in practical terms by the substitution of a machine for somebody's job, in unemployment and redundancy, but also in the debasement of something which is valuable in terms of the quality of life. It appears to be admitted that it is one of the main duties of any government to arrange its fiscal and economic policies so as to provide the strongest possible incentives to increased productivity, and at the same time it is agreed that undue emphasis on the production and sale of things which are unnecessary and perhaps even undesirable is one of the principal evils of the age. Anyone who appears to advocate technological change is likely to be branded as a thoughtless materialist, and anyone who opposes it as a sentimental traditionalist, or worse, as unable or unwilling to face the consequences of providing an acceptable standard of living for a whole people, instead of only for a privileged minority.

These contradictions and conflicts seem to be felt much more intensely in the United Kingdom than elsewhere. Indeed, dislike and resentment of technology is very often associated in people's minds with dislike and resentment of other nations, of the United States for example, which seem to be better able to adapt themselves to the conditions of contemporary society than we are. No doubt there is an historical reason for this. The memory of the excesses of the industrial revolution is still very much with us. Some of the dark satanic mills are still in production. Because the

21

industrial revolution came first to England, because it was associated directly with *laissez-faire* economics, at first untempered by the nineteenth-century evangelical conscience, the British experience of the price to be paid for industrial advance was far higher than elsewhere. In the imagination of many Englishmen to this day more industry means more slums, more slag-heaps, more prison-like factories swallowing up the countryside, more people engaged on dull routine occupations motivated only by the threat of starvation, or more recently by the bribe of higher wages.

The more obvious evils of the industrial revolution are now at last vanishing. And, as they vanish, a fashion for "industrial archaeology" appears as proof that you can be nostalgic about *anything*. In ten years or so, the worst of the slum housing will have disappeared; the standard of architecture and interior design of industrial buildings will be at least as high as and perhaps higher than any other contemporary construction; the waste products of industry, if not entirely eliminated, will at least be got out of sight, and doubtless the image of the industrial environment which they presented will gradually fade. But what about the image of industry as a social experience? Will it remain true that the industrial worker is seen as "a cog in the machine", not esteemed as an individual, thrown aside when no longer wanted, his working days spent in a soulless routine of repetitive labour, punctuated only occasionally by the profitless excitement of an industrial dispute?

It may even be supposed that as the direct manual element in industrial work becomes less and less, as hand tools are everywhere replaced by machine tools, as the concept of the craftsman is replaced by that of the technician, the working situation in industry will become still further degraded and depersonalized.

It is the first purpose of this chapter to argue that this view of the matter is totally wrong, that the replacement of the primitive technology of the industrial revolution by the scientific technology of to-day in fact provides a situation in which the workers—all of them at all levels— can be much more valued as persons, as individuals, all different but all "members one of another", and all bound together in mutual responsibility.

This suggestion is, I think, almost diametrically opposed to the common view of industry from outside, and to make it even partially credible would require a detailed examination of the evolution of ways of working in many industrial situations, far more than there is space for in one chapter. It is one of the obstacles to comprehension by those without direct experience that industries which appear not dissimilar from outside may in fact offer to their employees widely different conditions of work and social atmosphere. But it is worth while trying to describe in detail in one or two typical instances the effect of technological advance on what particular groups of employees are expected to do.

Let us consider first the kind of operation which most people would regard as typical of manufacturing industry. What has to be made is a large number of identical components; one of the main operations in manufacture has to be performed on a lathe.

The traditional organization for performing this operation is very simple. It consists of a number, say twenty, lathes arranged in rows in a workshop. Each lathe has its own operator, all of them performing an identical job. One man, the "chargehand", supervises the whole group. Now let us try to describe the arrangement which would be likely to supersede this traditional organization if the factory were modernized, or a new one built. The original twenty lathes are replaced by a much smaller number, perhaps four, automatic lathes controlled not by hand but by some form of electronic device, each working ten times as fast as a manually operated machine, so that the total output is doubled. Each automatic lathe needs only one operator; so that four operators in all are required, and it might be thought that the change contributes heavily to "technological redundancy". But to see whether it does or not we have to consider all the consequences of technological change, and not just the effect on the number of lathe operators.

The new organization is likely to look something like this:

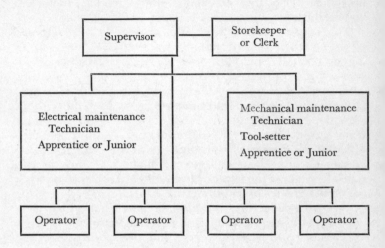

The effectiveness of the whole operation now depends not, as in the traditional system, on the effort put in by the individual operator—by and large the rate at which the automatic lathes run will be fixed by factors outside the control of the operator—but (a) on the smooth running of the organization for supplying material and taking away the finished product (hence the need for a "storekeeper"); and (b) still more important, on keeping the machines themselves and the electronic devices controlling them in working order with the fewest possible breakdowns and intervals for adjustment. They are of course far more complex and with many more items that can go wrong than a traditional lathe. Hence the need for electrical and mechanical maintenance men on the spot.

On the face of it, therefore, our doubled output has been achieved by eleven men instead of by twenty-one, but this also is an illusion. The change creates new opportunities and changes in the pattern of employment in a number of other ways.

First, because of the much increased cost of the machines, the firm will spend more of its income on capital goods, less on wages. In our illustration we can represent this by supposing that three of the men originally employed have gone off to work for a company making automatic lathes and control gear, where they take part in a not dissimilar pattern of employment.

Secondly, our greatly increased rate of output means that we need two more employees in office work, one of them on administration and management, and one for sales, marketing, and servicing. It is far easier to increase productivity in the actual processes of manufacture than in these ancillary activities. Similarly, a much more rapid rate of technical advance means that we must have a larger staff on research and on the design and development of new products, so we must allow for one extra job there also.

Thirdly, better holidays and shorter hours of work mean that on the average through the working year two of the twenty-one operators are, in the new régime, not available for work at all.

Finally, as we shall see in more detail later, a much higher average standard of education is called for in the new system, and so we must allow for one of our younger employees always to be absent on "day-release" and for one more to be not available because he is still a full-time student.

In all, therefore, the total number of jobs involved in the operation as a whole is the same as before.

Of course it may well be held that this kind of argument is altogether too facile; that the new programme has been distorted with the object of demonstrating that increasing sophistication in technology does not lead to unemployment, and of course a single illustration of this kind can provide no valid evidence on the question. But, on a larger scale, it is not difficult to find better evidence in the same direction. The nations which have serious unemployment problems at the present time are those which are relatively primitive in technology. It is true that there is a fair measure of unemployment in the United States, the example of all that is progressive" in industry, but even there a closer look suggests that it is only in the States which have not taken a proper share in the advance of industry, and among classes of the community, such as the Negroes, who have been artificially deprived of the necessary educational opportunity, that unemployment is anything more than a marginal problem. It is in India and Africa, which have not yet achieved their industrial revolutions, that unemployment on a gross scale persists.

A change of this kind usually means just as many jobs available, but the individuals concerned are not the same, and the nature of the work done is in a number of instances quite different in the two cases. The technical change has brought in its wake all sorts of changes in organizational and social structures, and it is these broader consequences which we must now examine.

Our original situation with the twenty operators each performing the same work under the direction of the charge-hand is in theory at least a competitive one. Payment is most likely to be wholly or partly on piece-rates, so that the most energetic and most tireless workers can in theory earn much above the average rate. In practice this supposedly competitive situation is very often deliberately made ineffective. The most able and vigorous workers choose to limit their output (and therefore their earnings) in order not to get too far away from the norm. Often enough, no doubt, they suspect with reason that too high earnings would simply produce a reduction in the standard rate for the job, so that everyone will be worse off. (On the other side of the fence, managements, by price-fixing and cartel arrangements, combine to frustrate the theoretical benefit of competition from the consumers' point of view.) Nevertheless, although there may be this kind of concealed understanding, no operator is required to assist any other. Indeed, no communication of any kind is necessary between them. If he is capable of reading a hundred or two hundred words of instruction, an operator can perfectly well be deaf and dumb. If any worker chooses on a particular day to stay in bed, or go to the races, the loss of output amounts to his contribution only; none of the other nineteen operators is affected in any way. If, as a result of a slackening in demand, no work was forthcoming, the operators could be dismissed at short notice. The charge-hand had usually himself been one of the operators, distinguished not by greater technical ability or better education, but by willingness to accept a position involving leadership and tact in order to prevent unnecessary friction. He alone has any responsibility for the work of any other person.

None of these considerations applies in the new situation. Of the eleven workers shown in the diagram all are mutually dependent in a variety of ways, and must be constantly co-operating with one another if the system is to work smoothly. Each of the four operators must be aware what the others are doing so that a complicated schedule of operation, repairs, and maintenance can be adhered to. Each of them must have a relationship of confidence and understanding with the specialist technicians, and the supervisor. If one of them makes a mistake, putting one machine out of action, the loss of production is immediately one-quarter of the total, and may easily be more. It may be that there is some kind of system of payment by results, but it is almost certainly a group system so that the wages of the whole group move up or down together, and no member of the group can do well at the expense of any other member. All of them are in some sense responsible for the others. If work is short, the management will probably do its best to avoid dismissing anyone, in part perhaps for altruistic reasons, or to avoid earning the company a bad name, but also for reasons of direct self-interest. A good deal of money has been invested in training these men in the much more complicated tasks they are now doing. If they are discharged, they will very likely go to work for a competitor and may not come back when better times come. If a harmonious team is broken up, it may be impossible to re-create it.

Within the group there is little competition. The technicians are specialists with special experience and training, and the operators cannot take their places without long

C

preparation. The supervisor is probably better—or at least more generally—educated than the others. He may be a young graduate or the holder of a higher qualification from a Technical College. If he leaves or is promoted to wider responsibility his place will be taken by a newcomer with similar attainments.

The case of the lathe operators is, of course, only one among many other illustrations which might have been chosen. The same kind of thing happens in fields which are not directly connected with manufacturing industry. Let us take as a second illustration what might happen in the accounting section of a large organization. Until recently there would have been rows of clerks making out bills and receipts, doing the arithmetic of the firm, all engaged independently on more or less the same kind of work. Such an office now has, or ought to have, a computer, which if properly programmed and looked after will calculate and print on paper all the information which was formerly laboriously written out by hand or typed (and much more besides), in a fraction of the time. The computer itself, doing a much better job, needs perhaps half as many people to work it (again a mutually dependent group of programmers, operators, and maintenance technicians) as the original payroll of clerks. But the jobs which have disappeared in the accounting office have been re-created elsewhere, in the much more precise and far-sighted management which a quicker supply of information makes possible, in the manufacture of computers, in increased educational needs, in greater leisure. Here also the march of technology makes the job much more varied and interesting, and also much more complex and dependent on human relationships than the old method was.[1]

[1] Is it too imaginative to discern an analogy with the kind of evolution now beginning to take place in the organization of the Church itself, in which the old structure of one man, the "Minister" in charge of a number of other people, the "Congregation", all equal and having the same kind of duties, is replaced by a much more complicated structure of many people, social workers, teachers, fund-raisers, ministers of the sacraments, evangelists, philosophers, scholars, and musicians, all with "mutual responsibility" for one another.

The traditional structure of industry, with "management" supported by a limited number of specialist and technical staff on one side, and "labour", organized in a single Union, on the other, represented the old organization perfectly well. The task of the Union was to secure the best possible rates of pay and conditions of work for a single class, the operators, the clerks, etc. The tendency, inherent in Union constitutions, to give the greatest prominence to the claims of the most numerous and worst paid workers exactly coincided with the social need to meet which they were devised. The chain of command and function on the management side was equally clear, even if there was often undue reluctance to delegate authority.

In the new situation, this traditional structure serves very badly. If we adhere to the old demarcations, this small group responsible for the automatic lathes will contain members of the Amalgamated Engineering Union, of the Electrical Trades Union, of one or more "white-collar" Unions. Unless a certain amount of flexibility is permitted; unless, for example, we allow the boundary between what the technicians do and what the operators do to become very blurred, there is likely to be so much waste of time and duplication of effort that much of the economic advantage of the change will be lost. There are strong reasons for getting rid of the old pattern altogether, and adopting a different one in which everyone working in a particular industry belongs to the same Union. Of course, such an "industrial" Union will have to face entirely new problems. Instead of being primarily concerned with a basic wage-rate for its members, it will have to interest itself in a great variety of different salaries and wages, and ought in theory to evolve a set of principles of its own for determining the relativities between different occupations and classes of membership. Conflicts within a single Union, or between one Union and another, instead of between the Union on the one hand and the employer on the other are clearly possible.

Plainly also in the new situation, the old distinction between "staff" on the one hand and "labour" on the other

rapidly becomes untenable. It is very difficult to draw any
kind of sensible frontier between the two. The old distinction
between manual and non-manual work will not do. (Is a
computer operator manual or non-manual, an electronic
technician or a copy-typist?) Nor will the idea that people
above a given rate of pay are "staff", and those below that
figure are "labour". If a mistake by the operator of a huge
machine will cost you thousands, you will be very ready to
pay what is necessary to reduce the chance of a mistake to a
minimum. But even if such a line can be drawn after a
fashion, it serves no useful purpose, since, increasingly, there
is no point in having different "terms and conditions of
service" for the two categories, for example, to pay one set
of people weekly in cash, and another set of people monthly
by cheque.

If technological change makes difficulties for the traditional kind of Trades Union structure, it makes difficulties
also on the management side. For one thing it makes a clear
"chain of command" very difficult to devise. What are the
respective duties and responsibilities of "line management"
and specialists and technical experts? How can demand,
represented by the order book, and by the clamour of the
sales staff for firm delivery dates, be co-ordinated with supply,
represented by the need to use the available machinery in
the most economical way? How can the accountants, who by
and large have been trained to think that success is measured
by the profit at the end of the year, agree with engineers,
who believe that success means that their product serves the
purpose better than any other? True, in the large company
there is an organization chart apparently defining who is
responsible for what, and who is entitled to give instructions
to whom, but newcomers will soon find that the real situation
is very different from what the chart suggests. To a large
extent the organization is self-directing. What is done is
what the technical conditions of the situation require. If a
particular group of workers can in a last resort bring a whole
factory—or a whole industry—to a standstill, then decisions
which seem to them intolerable cannot be made, whatever

the organization chart says. If the machines operated in a particular way regularly break down, then it is useless to tell people to operate them in that way. Just as the new technology calls for a much higher level of voluntary co-operation among the workers on the shop floor (as well as a higher level of technical understanding), so it also requires from management a much clearer appreciation of the real nature of human relationships, and a deeper understanding of the conditions under which people work well together.

When all these difficulties are envisaged, it is not difficult to appreciate the reasons for the reluctance with which industry ("both sides of industry") faces up to technological change. It is all too easy to think that in cases in which the economic advantage of making a change is not very large or very certain, as in most cases it will not be, it is wiser to continue along traditional lines. But there is one factor, and it ought to be the decisive one, which has not appeared in the argument so far. Whatever its difficulties from the point of view of shop stewards or managers, whatever its extra demands on our patience from special interests or general ill will, most of us feel instinctively that we are at bottom much happier, and in the proper sense of the words, much better off, in the complex human situation which modern technology requires, than in the over-simplified and regimented uniformities of the old organization. The term "mutual responsibility" has only quite recently become part of the common vocabulary of the Church. But it has been part of the accepted ideal of life for the working man at least since the industrial revolution and perhaps long before that. His readiness to accept the principle that all must be prepared to sacrifice themselves to prevent the victimization of one, his rejection of the competitive situation even when attempts were made to build it into the system of payment, to which reference has already been made, the spontaneous appearance of coherent, if informal, working groups in industries like mining and the docks: all these things are evidence that when the opportunity is offered for men to work together in a responsible way, it will be taken.

In these pages we have been talking of cases in which it is
the character of the technique which dominates the situation. Often, this must be the case. All computers are broadly
the same, all really advanced and automatically controlled
machine tools are broadly the same. The principles on
which they are designed determine the kind of work they
do, and the kinds of people needed to get the best out of
them. But in many other cases, the situation is not as simple
as that. We have a choice of industrial techniques which
require more skilled and specialized workers, or less; we
have a choice between a factory organization which calls for
people more able to co-operate in a team with mutual understanding, or less so. At present, the information on which
such choices are based is very inadequate. Very often they
are made on not much more than the "hunch"—or the
prejudice—of a works manager. Plainly, people who take the
view that the social environment of industry is important,
that factory work should be as satisfying to the individual
worker at every level as it is possible to make it, have a duty
not only to speak out as clearly as possible in these issues,
but also to do what they can to provide the evidence on
which proper choices can be made. Of course, in part, what
kind of industrial organization is best depends on the pre-
vailing standards of education. But it depends much less
than is generally supposed on standards at the top, and
much more on standards at the middle and lower middle
levels. The revolution which is now going on in English
education, a revolution which means that in twenty years
perhaps one man in five employed in industry will have a
degree, and which insists on organizing secondary education
not solely with the aim of developing the brains of the ablest
in the most economical possible way, but with the needs of
the average as the prime concern, this revolution, although
it has come about for quite different reasons, represents the
first real attempt to provide what is wanted by an industrial
nation.

Nothing has been of greater interest to people concerned
with education for industry in the last thirty years than to

see how opinion among industrialists themselves has changed about the kind and amount of education which is required by their recruits. Not much more than a generation ago most of them regarded apprenticeship in the strict sense of the word, "learning by doing", as the only proper preparation for an industrial career. State education was useful enough for teaching people to read and write and do arithmetic, but when that much was achieved the sooner the boys began to learn the job on the shop floor the better. A minimum number of engineering graduates might be accepted on the general theory that some of them might later prove to have the qualities needed for management, though the work they did and their rates of pay in the early stages were not very different from those of an apprentice of fifteen. Only a minority of employers thought it worth while to encourage their young people to try to improve their qualifications through evening classes, and almost none was prepared to grant "day-release" for the same purpose.

When this attitude began to change, what industry wanted from the educational system was at first defined in the narrowest terms—training to do a job, often a job very specifically defined. Technical college courses were devised in many cases simply to reproduce as closely as possible the conditions of the factory. (So far as the technical side of the work was concerned, that is; the human relationships in the factory could not be adequately reproduced in the colleges, and this was one of the weaknesses of the system.) To transfer the instructional side of an apprenticeship to a special institution is plainly an advantage in some ways. The instruction can be much more systematically planned and can be carried out by professional instructors. Even in the universities the influence of industry, although a good deal modified by the idiosyncrasies of academics, was always exerted in the direction of making courses narrowly vocational.

The position to-day could hardly be more different. An employer who does not grant "day-release" for further education, not just to a selected few but to all his employees in the appropriate age range, is regarded in the best industrial circles as something of a backwoodsman. The employment of graduates is so much a symbol of an enlightened management policy that the universities themselves must try to advise their young men, not always very wisely, as to which jobs will really stretch their abilities and which are mere window-dressing. And courses for technicians and others just below graduate level are under continuous fire as being too few, too short, and too narrowly conceived.

If industry's assessment of how much education it needs has changed radically, its concept of the kind of education it needs is changing even more. No doubt this concept is still very indeterminate, and not yet well thought out, but there are plenty of indications of the direction in which things are moving. When, a few years ago, the diploma in technology was introduced into the leading technical colleges as an alternative qualification at degree level, it was the industrialists who insisted that all such courses should contain a substantial element of "liberal studies"—a phrase which at the time apparently meant any study which had nothing to do with the technological problems of industry. The universities now are under no pressure whatever to increase the vocational content of their courses. On the contrary, they are all the time receiving anxious inquiries as to whether the "factual" (i.e. the technical) element in their courses has not become so overloaded that there is no time for "general reading" or for "the development of personal qualities".

We have here yet another field in which traditional British attitudes seem ill adapted to contemporary needs. What is at bottom meant by the industrialist talking about "personal qualities" is the ability to work well in a group, to be a good member of a team, and so on—just the qualities which are needed to make the best use of modern technology. But at least in the more academic branches of the school system, the grammar schools and the public schools, team work has been something strictly confined to the sports field; when it appears in the classroom it is called cheating. It is as though these schools, whose general pattern and ethos date from the age of *laissez-faire*, have preserved from that time the idea that in the serious business of life the only quality which counts is competitiveness. Everything is directed towards an examination, the essential purpose of which is to put people in an order of merit. It is one of the sad things in recent educational history that the secondary modern schools, which were originally designed to be quite free of this kind of competition to provide a milieu in which children could learn about the problems of co-operating constructively in a society of manageable size,[2] have found the traditional pressures too strong, and have been compelled to follow step by step (and necessarily some distance behind) the practices they were supposed to replace.

This doctrine, that education is not something in which individual ability and application is the only thing which counts and the only thing to be nurtured, is of course still anathema to most British academics. It seems so inevitably an attack on the concepts of "quality" and "standards" which have been the hallmark of success for schools and universities for so long. Indeed, if universal competition and classification is the price one must pay for the maintenance of standards, then for my own part I would say it was worth paying. But it seems to me that a time has come when we have to re-examine once again the question of whether what is essential in what we mean by "standards", what is relevant in what we mean by "quality", cannot be preserved and enhanced in ways which give much more emphasis to the collective, the social, and the co-operative elements in education.[3]

[2] An indication of the widespread feeling among young people that work ought to be something to be done co-operatively and not individually or competitively is the almost universal demand among undergraduates for more "seminars" and "group tutorials" in which a number of students argue out their difficulties together, as opposed either to the lecture system (in which it appears to them one man can try to impose his view on others) or the Oxbridge "individual tutorial" system which, since each student is supposed to work alone, can be made essentially competitive.

[3] Many British educationalists take the line that the dangers of stressing the "social" element in education are exemplified by American experience.

There is ample evidence then that the technological society is an educated society, indeed a society in which education in the broadest sense of the word, not simply as training in technical expertise, is distributed much more fairly and widely than in any previous society. This most of us would surely regard as one of its principal advantages. But even this has its dangers. Will the educated society prove to be as susceptible to class divisions as those that it replaces? Will people become—are they already becoming—as snobbish about their education as they were formerly about their birth or their money? Plainly, there is a risk that this will happen, but education is, after all, essentially a self-critical process. Perhaps a really well-educated people would be sufficiently clear-sighted to see that such social divisions are all essentially destructive, and sufficiently disinterested to draw the appropriate conclusions.

A second risk to which attention has often been drawn is that such a society might find no place at all for people of less than average intelligence. It is usually easy to make a machine which can do a routine and repetitive job. Before long there will be no routine and repetitive jobs left, and what then is to happen to people who are incapable of anything more than routine and repetition?

The risk that a situation of this kind might develop undoubtedly exists in theory. There is no real evidence that it has ever done so in practice. There have been times and places in which serious "unskilled" unemployment existed alongside a shortage of "skilled" personnel. In such cases what has been lacking is not ability among the unskilled, but the educational provision necessary to help them to become skilled. (Of course, in some cases obstacles have been deliberately erected in the path of the unskilled in order to preserve the scarcity value of the skilled.) The most obstinate problems of "redundancy" are not those of finding a new

And indeed the idea of designing courses for schoolchildren on how to make oneself socially successful or how to behave towards the opposite sex fills us with horror. But such extravagances are a long way away from the experience of working together towards the common intellectual purpose.

occupation for the unskilled, but those which arise when demand for particular kinds of highly skilled work decreases too sharply. And many such cases occur for a reason to which we have already referred, that twenty or thirty years ago technological skills were often built up on too narrow an educational base.

This chapter was supposed to be about the impact of technology on our society as a whole. It has turned out to be almost entirely about its impact on our working lives, and particularly on the working lives of those of us who make a living in industry. They are the people who are most directly affected by technological change; perhaps it is not unfair to say that they are the people to whose interests and welfare the Church ought now to be directing much of its thought, since they have in the past been so much neglected. But technology has consequences beyond our working lives, consequences for social mobility, for the family, for relationships between the sexes and between the generations. Some of these consequences can be discerned only dimly, some are still quite unknown, some have implications so profound that even a superficial discussion would need many more chapters. They must be left for another occasion and for another writer. But there is perhaps one feature which is so universal and so evident that something must be said about it, and that is the effect of technology on leisure and the use of leisure.

The full impact of technology in giving people more leisure is still partly concealed. It is concealed because the system of overtime payment gives people a strong motive for spreading their work over as long a period as possible. But one may think that as more and more people move on to a salary basis, as opposed to an hourly rate, this tendency will gradually disappear. It is concealed also because housing shortages (and city traffic!) mean that people spend more and more time travelling to and from their work. But one may hope, even if faintly, that better town planning and better location of industry will reverse this trend also. In our time we have seen the five-day week become almost universal,

and it cannot be long before most people have as much time
for leisure (genuine leisure, not counting time for commut-
ing and for the necessary business of eating and sleeping) as
they spend on their work.

Some people profess to see a threat in this tendency also.
"Satan finds some mischief for idle hands to do." It seems to
me that these fears are easily refuted. For centuries there
has been a leisured class of people who had all their time,
not just half of it, free of work. (In fact this class is now a
smaller proportion of the population than it has been for
many generations.) There is no evidence that this leisured
class was on the average from a Christian point of view either
better or worse than those who had to work for their living.
A man who has very little leisure, like a man who has very
little money, may not lay it out, in the opinion of the
sagacious, to the best advantage, but who can blame him for
that? Up to now the evidence is that people who now for the
first time have adequate leisure use it in ways which, if
uninspired, are by no means useless, in "do-it-yourself"
improvements to houses and gardens, in attempts to overcome by foreign travel the disadvantage of living on an
island, in searching hopefully, if unsystematically, for a new
art and a new literature which speaks to the contemporary
condition.

The pity is that so much more is possible. A man can have
a second profession in addition to that by which he makes
his living, and his attainments in this second profession can
be as high as in the first. He can be free if he wishes to make
his work in his second profession entirely unpaid, rewarding
him only in the enrichment of his life and of the society to
which he belongs. He may give himself to social service, to
the arts, to education, to the ministry of the Church, not in
the amateur way in which we have been accustomed to think
of our spare-time activities, but on a basis of equality with
a "full-time" professional. And if these are activities which
have in the past been associated in our minds with a small
educated class, it is this class which must grow till it includes the greater part, if not the whole, of our society.

This chapter began by pointing out how conflicting and confused were the accepted views about technology and what it can do, and how difficult was the task of writing about it. It can well conclude by pointing out yet another difficulty, that at a time when pessimism is the order of the day, and despair the fashionable attitude, a technologist cannot prevent optimism breaking through. Hard work, hard thinking, and patience, the industrious virtues, are not the answer to all the problems of suffering humanity, but they are the answer to some of them. Some of the sorrows, some of the evils which have obstructed our path and blinded our vision over so many generations, it is within our power to remove for good, and to fail to do for ourselves what God has made it possible for us to do is deliberately to reject his will.

4 Race, Culture, Nationalism

Philip Mason

A prudent person would hesitate to entrust a lamb to the guardianship of a wolf, however firmly he might believe that one day the wolf shall dwell with the lamb and the leopard lie down with the kid. There is an inescapable Christian dilemma: How can one combine the irrational optimism of God with a prudent and realistic assessment of what experience suggests is likely to occur in human affairs? All men are the sons of God, but there is a strong probability that in certain kinds of circumstance groups of men will behave to each other like children of the devil.

The emphasis is on groups. Even the bestiality and ferocity of war is starred from time to time by kindness between individuals. Between individuals, it is easier to see that the supreme gamble of trust must be taken wherever possible, though even here it would, to take an extreme case, surely not be right to send your little daughter for a walk in the country with a psychopathic murderer. But between groups, the dilemma is inescapable and daily more pressing. It concerns minorities and the creation of minorities by migration; should you put a muzzle on the wolf and make him more savage and more frustrated? Or should you trust the wolf and let the lamb take his chance?

It may be assumed that anyone who has read this book so far is in general sympathy with the Christian belief that all men share the fatherhood of God. He will be quite clear that to deny members of a minority formal civic equality or equal opportunities for education, employment, or housing is a sin. But he may find it a good deal more difficult to decide what is right about immigration.

Progress in human knowledge has come through the mixing of human groups, while for individuals a great enrichment of experience can come from meeting people of other races and cultures. We should like, then, to see every barrier down, free immigration everywhere. As Christians we recognize that to say yes to Australians and not to Indians is hurtful and invidious. Again, it is clearly selfish to keep our prosperity for ourselves alone. But while in some places mixing of very different peoples has taken place peacefully —or at least has reached a peaceful stage—in others hatred and malice have flared up and people have been killed, hurt, humiliated. Ought we to take precautions to avoid this? What are the special ingredients in the kind of situation that goes wrong?

Fear is perhaps the chief of these ingredients; fear is a fact, not immutable, but to be disregarded at peril. But it is at least as dangerous to give way to fear and endeavour to keep races or groups apart as it is to ignore it and hope for the best. South Africa is not a happier country than British Guiana; has Australia done more than postpone the problem? *Can* we do anything to prevent strife, even if we ought? I have been writing as though we were all statesmen or even more—almighty disposers of the affairs of men. In practice very few people can influence policy, and the sphere of possible action open even to statesmen is limited. What can an ordinary person do about this and what kind of attitude should he adopt?

White Australia—the admission of commonwealth immigrants to Britain—independence for Southern Rhodesia—Britain's behaviour to South Africa—these are one set of questions to which this dilemma applies; another set, somewhat in the past for practical purposes, is the fate of minorities after independence, the Nagas in India, the Tiv in Nigeria, the Southern Sudanese. It is impossible to deal with all of these in a short space; as an illustration, I shall put special emphasis in this chapter on Britain.

Within the memory of any Englishman of forty or over, Muslims and Hindus have slaughtered each other in India,

federal force has been used to compel the attendance of
Negroes at school in Little Rock, police have opened fire on
a peaceful crowd at Sharpeville in South Africa, and in
Notting Hill young men have gone out armed with iron bars
for what they described as a "nigger hunt". These are all
symptoms of a disease in which fear is a component. There
is a special anger in fear when it seems likely that past
exploitation is coming to an end; there is another kind of
fear when cracks begin to appear in an imperial cement,
which has held together quite different peoples but which is
now seen to be about to dissolve. Fear too is felt at the
ferment of changing values when people pour in from the
countryisde to great industrial towns, when tribal life breaks
up, and when there seems nothing to put in the place of the
old tribal or rural standards of conduct. All these fears
sometimes take on a sharper edge when the difference between the groups concerned is marked by some visible
physical characteristic. But this is not always the case;
nothing could be much sharper than what Hindus and
Muslims did to each other.

All this might seem to suggest that it would be prudent to
keep people apart, and this is the argument for Australian
policy and for those who want complete restriction on
immigration to Britain. Some people will reject this angrily
—but if Australia had admitted a large Indian or Chinese
population in Victorian times, is it not likely that white
Australians would have become *herrenvolk*, faced with the
same kind of problem as South Africa? The case is quite
different once immigration has taken place; *within* a nation
State there can be no question at all where duty lies. Segregation is morally wrong because it is humiliating; it happens
that there are arguments of prudence against it too. It is
difficult to arrange and expensive in terms of wasted energy
and wasted opportunity. Between States, the case is quite
different; some degree of separation is easier to arrange; at
first sight the prudent arguments are strong on the side of
separation—at least for the richer countries. You want to
keep up wages and standards of living and of health, you

want to avoid conflict and bitterness over housing and mixed marriages, you dread having to see in your beloved country hoses and police dogs and sit-in strikes. Other people's poverty and squalor is much easier to bear at a safe distance. Even the argument of good neighbourliness is ambiguous; are you likely to be better friends with your neighbour if you keep her subjects out or if you let them in and discriminate against them, building up bitterness and hate? Can you be sure that this is not what you will do? The arguments on the other side are not prudent; they involve courage. They are ultimately either Christian or based on assumptions derivative from Christian values. Isolation means stagnation, selfishness, and death; it implies arrogance, it involves humiliation. It denies the Incarnation; it denies the divine in man. Stated in general terms, the dilemma is complete; God's optimism stands starkly opposed to man's realism. It needs more analysis.

The history of mankind has been one of the alternate isolation and intermixing of populations. Their physique, during many thousands of years, and their culture, in a few decades, has responded to each isolated environment. When they meet, their meeting changes the environment, and both are modified again in response to what has happened. This process is not dissimilar from the alternate inbreeding and outbreeding practised by the human breeder of plants and animals. It has been the machinery of progress.

To-day, if we avoid blowing ourselves to radio-active dust, there can surely be no doubt that the emphasis is bound to be more closely on meeting and mixing. The complexities of industry and finance make us more dependent on each other than ever before. Communications are quicker and easier; the journey from London to Accra takes about the same time to-day as the journey to Edinburgh sixty years ago. More and more people will stream into towns, more and more people will—if they are permitted—cross seas and deserts in order to improve their lot on the other side. This will mean that the contacts are between people who in appearance, as well as in past culture, are more sharply differentiated than was

D

the case in the past. Over this close involvement hangs suspended a supreme leveller, the Bomb, and from this the only escape lies in much closer international interdependence.

It need hardly be stressed that mankind is all one species, the various strains breeding together freely unless prevented by legal or religious sanctions, and that the biological differences of skin colour, hair formation, and bone structure seem to have little relevance for survival in a modern environment and much less significance for human relationships than the cultural differences, the values and the perceptions about human behaviour. But hereditary physical differences have a greater *permanence* than cultural traits because they are carried on into later generations and they are sometimes *supposed* to have a deeper significance than can so far be scientifically demonstrated. The evidence seems to indicate that while hostility to strangers clearly has deep roots in human nature, hostility based on colour as a special factor is a matter of culture and upbringing rather than of instinct.

In spite of all these humane and rational considerations, the fact remains that human beings behave towards each other like devils. Why? There is one fact in common to the situations so far mentioned—Hindu–Muslim riots in 1947, Little Rock, Sharpeville, Notting Hill. Everywhere one group of persons has looked on the other not as individuals, but in generalized terms. One group has a fixed mental picture of the other. "They" are dirty, over-sexed, irresponsible, cruel—and so it does not matter what you do to them. There is nothing new about this habit of putting people into mental pigeon-holes, making fixed mental pictures or stereotypes; the story of the good Samaritan was meant to jerk Jewish thinking out of the general stereotypes of the priest, the Levite, and the Samaritan. It hardly needs emphasis to-day that it is the frightened mind that most persistently takes refuge in this habit of pigeon-holing. At times, of course, it may look like laziness rather than fear, but even then it is probably fear of taking trouble, of the adventure of thinking something out for oneself, that makes the habit.

Social research has shown that hostile attitudes—what are sometimes called negative attitudes—to Jews and Negroes are strongest among those who have risen or fallen in the social scale since their childhood. Both those who have moved up and those who have moved down are uncertain, frightened of the environment in which they now find themselves, eager to assert their own worth. Both meet fear and uncertainty by hostility to a group thought of as "them". The basic cause of hostility may be an irrational self-defence but it *wants* to be rational. It will seize on a rational excuse where it can. This kind of fear is seen very clearly over housing. "This used to be a decent street once, but now *they* have moved in"—this was a remark made by Irish Protestants about Irish Catholics in Liverpool, but it might just as well have been said, and in fact is daily said, by the white inhabitants of Birmingham (Warwickshire) about West Indians.

Human nature is constantly in search of support and self-justification. If no support is to be found in God, it will be sought in the esteem of one's fellow-creatures. And, if that esteem is not forthcoming to the degree that the Ego feels is proper—and it seldom is—it will be sought in membership of a gang. The more uncertain he is of his own value in the eyes of his fellow-beings, the more Ego will be inclined to fall back on some classification which he feels justifies him in feeling superior.

It is therefore realistic to recognize that there are likely to be people in any society who will be hostile to any minority, and particularly to a minority that looks different. If the society as a whole is puzzled, frustrated, and unhappy, suffering under a sense of injustice—as Germany was after the First World War—then the likelihood of open hostility to a minority is greater. Is there a similar, if lesser danger, for a nation which has lost an Empire and is still looking for a rôle? In the two generations since the Diamond Jubilee, Britain has had to adjust herself to a very different position in world affairs. However that question is answered, there is no doubt that shortages bring out a new sharpness in what may otherwise be only a vague jealousy.

Another chapter in this book has dealt with the confrontation between rich nations and poor. An important aspect of this is closely linked with ideas about race. It results from the technical superiority in the last century of men of Western European stock; during the last years of the reign of Queen Victoria and the years leading up to the First World War this produced political dominance over almost the whole world. To this dominance the reaction of the rest has been sharp, and there has been built up in the minds of each group of peoples stereotypes or mental pictures of the other which it will take generations to live down. Any man of middle age to-day from the Western nations is fortunate if he has not imbibed during his early youth a derogatory picture of people with a different pigmentation from his own. He is likely to think of them as above all *poor*—and with that poverty goes in his mind dirt, disease, idleness, untruthfulness, and, needless to say, a vicious sexuality, a repulsive kind of cruelty. Looking from amongst the poverty of his people towards the West, the Asian or the African sees white men who are powerful and rich in the kind of sense so often unfavourably pictured in the New Testament. With this picture of power and riches goes an impression of people too busy to be polite, unscrupulous in making others work for them, proud, cold, deceitful—and, needless to say, vicious in their sexuality, repellent in their cruelty.

These stereotypes will be the harder to overcome because there is an element of truth in both. The poor are often undernourished and with undernourishment often goes infestation with parasites. This means apathy—and apathy seems like idleness to a man who is well fed. If you are poor and powerless, you are likely to be frightened and untruthful. The rich are often so concerned with *things* that they have no time for *people*; they are apt to manipulate people for their own purposes—and this too will lead to untruthfulness. Whether you are rich or poor, if you think of another group of people as simply "they", you are apt to be cruel to them, and if one of "them" is the target of your sexuality you are apt to be cold, impersonal, and perhaps brutal.

Of course there have also been more favourable stereotypes, such as that of the kind master and the faithful servant. These too contained a basis of truth, but they are not found so often now, and there is a special bitterness of the kind master whose faithful servant has proved ungrateful and another of the faithful servant whose trust has been misplaced.

It was to meet associations of this kind that immigrants began to come to Britain in large numbers in the late fifties and early sixties. If they came from the West Indies, as many of them did, they believed that they were British and were shocked to find that to most English people they were merely coloured strangers. Indians and Pakistanis did not share this particular illusion; though less susceptible to bitterness on this account, they differed more from the host community in that they spoke different languages and belonged to different faiths. The English, mildly hostile to all strangers, like to think of themselves as tolerant and hospitable; they have been somewhat shocked to find that they are not, and their first instinct has been to deny that any problem exists.

A cycle of development has often shown itself in most of the areas in Britain where immigrants have settled. At first, a few immigrants arrive, and if they happen to look different, they are objects of not unfriendly curiosity and sometimes kindly interest. But this initial honeymoon period may easily change if numbers increase too rapidly. This is not to suggest that there is any magic proportion at which the change takes place; it is partly a matter of the pace of new arrivals and the time they take to settle down, and partly a matter of the readiness of the host community to accustom themselves to the strangers. Local leadership on both sides plays a big part.

If leadership is of the wrong kind, or not sufficiently decisive, a point may be reached where hostility and resentment among the local inhabitants become strong. Sometimes difficulties are real; differences of social custom can be trying at close quarters. On the other hand, stories quite without foundation are sometimes alleged; more often a fragment of truth is exaggerated or the true reason for behaviour misunderstood. Sometimes each group fails to realize how the other is placed. For example, many people speak of the grasping immigrant landlord. But few realize the circumstances which often lie behind the kind of rents that are charged for limited accommodation. The immigrant in any community, and whatever his colour, finds it difficult to obtain rented accommodation: in Britain if he is coloured, he finds it more difficult still and he has to pay more for it than a native citizen. He is therefore driven to buy a house as soon as he can. When he has saved enough money to start his search for a house in earnest he is often sold one at above the market value; agents sometimes tell vendors to put up the price because there is a West Indian in the market. Having acquired the option, he has to raise the rest of the money. What he cannot borrow from his friends has to come from a mortgage, and here again he is usually made to pay higher interest than a native on shorter terms of repayment—sometimes repayment in seven to ten years. Thus when he gets the house he is crippled by a debt which is far beyond his means. He can only meet his commitments by bringing in as many people as he can and charging them at exorbitant rates.

Housing is always a sore point. It is easy to argue with negative crudity: "There are not enough houses anyhow. Why did 'they' have to come and make more people and the shortage worse?" It is a much more complex argument —and one that demands knowledge of facts not easy to discover—that housing depends largely on the capacity of the building industry which depends on labour. In a specialized industrial society, a man in the building trade must be assumed to produce more housing-space than he occupies; there are less than two per cent of immigrants in Britain while far more than two per cent of the building trade are immigrants. It may therefore well be that the housing shortage is being improved by the presence of immigrants.

But when all is said, no sensible person can doubt that

there are real difficulties on both sides in the way of living alongside people from a different culture. That many of the difficulties are based on misconception and misunderstanding does not alter their reality. What can be done to speed up the process towards the third stage in race relations, which may occur or may not, that of settling down together?

In the first place, it is as well to be clear what one is thinking of. It is convenient to make a distinction between assimilation—by which I mean complete absorption, the way the Huguenots disappeared into English Society—and integration, in which a minority group retains its separate identity for many purposes, while its individual members can mix in the larger society without any stigma or difficulty for other purposes. It must surely be the last for which we are aiming. We surely do not want the Sikh or the Muslim to abandon his faith and culture and to be merged in a faceless and unidentifiable mass. We do want each member of these communities to be able to go to school and get a job or a house without there being any discrimination against him.

Throughout this chapter the part played by fear has been stressed. Fear of losing a house or a job, fear of being demeaned in the eyes of the neighbours, fear of some invasion of one's privacy, fear of the loss of a secure unchallenged position on the white side—all these have been ingredients in racial hostility. On the other side, there has been fear of a rebuff, fear of some patronizing and condescending attitude, resentment at past exploitation and fear that it might be renewed in another form; all this has been mixed with a determination not to borrow an identity, not to borrow a way of life, but to achieve something distinctive of one's own. White fear of losing an advantage dovetails together with the mixed fears and resentments on the other side like two halves of a jigsaw puzzle; each is dependent on the other. And of course for every individual, the best way of dealing with fear is to go to meet it; to get to know someone who is thought of as one of "them" may well be the quickest way of answering the problem. But to say this or to say that everyone ought to recognize the fatherhood of God is not enough; it is to be profoundly unrealistic not to recognize that many will not go to meet their fear, will forget God once again. So we are back at the initial dilemma.

We must be clear about the kind of society we want. It is one built on the relationship described by St Paul, in which all are members one of another and play their different parts, as hand, ear, and eye, each with something different to do, but all suffering if one is hurt. But with his eyes fixed on this idea, a Christian must at the same time recognize that progress of any kind from a static and communal form of society—rural or tribal—to one that is individual, competitive, and open is always accompanied by ferment and usually by pain. He will believe that, even though there is loss when a tribal or rural society, with all the satisfactions it had, breaks up, the loss must be faced and endured with the hope of something better eventually emerging. He will therefore be radically opposed to any attempt to put back the clock. He will be unconvinced by arguments that "we ought to have stayed longer" in the countries of Africa, because he will recognize that progress, agonizing though it may be, can take place only if people feel they are responsible for their own destiny.

He will recognize, too, that perhaps the greatest wrong white people have done has been the assumption that "everything worth while is to be associated with whiteness, things like goodness, beauty, even God . . ." The words are a Jamaican's; he goes on to point out that this assumption condemns the non-white to permanent inferiority, from which he can escape only by aggressive assertion of the opposite creed, that only blackness is good. Once this is recognized, it becomes apparent that if discrimination and segregation are sins, so too is patronage, the attitude of: "You'd hardly know he wasn't an Englishman to hear him talk", the assumption that we can wholly assimilate, that the highest good is to be assimilated.

He will recognize too that to meet people of another culture, not as faithful servants but as equals, is a challenge, a privilege, and an opportunity, that it is in the end a sin to turn back from an opportunity. And yet—if what for me is an opportunity means hurt for someone else? In England it is the middle-class intellectual who sees race as a challenge, it is the people in a poor tenement house who have to make the painful adjustments. This does not alter the principle, it guides and determines it.

There is no easy answer, only a narrow and difficult road between excesses on either side. It would be unrealistic and sentimental to pretend that prejudice does not exist in England; to ignore it might lead to more Notting Hills, would almost certainly lead to growing bitterness. Control of immigration is therefore necessary; some increased strictness of control until the various groups of newcomers and the host community have had time to get used to each other. But to *stop* immigration would be the surrender of a principle. It would be giving in to fear, the refusal of a challenge, the assertion that whites have nothing to learn, that white is always best.

Thinking of South Africa, the Christian is bound to see a situation produced by fallen man from which there can be no solution without agony for all. Violence by the Government is taking place now, and in human terms there seems no way in which it can be ended except by further violence, leading to anarchy and prolonged misery. Can I acquiesce in what is unquestionably wrong to avoid anarchy? Can I calculate the precise weight of human misery involved in *apartheid* and put it in the balance against another calculated, but hypothetical, weight of misery that will result from revolution? The only Christian answer must be that I cannot act unless I am myself involved, that I must not act except at my own expense. But I cannot be detached; the degree of involvement must determine my action.

In Britain, decisions in respect of the internal situation are less agonizing. There can be no question that every one of us is involved in the acts of our Government. Everyone can learn something of the problem and have an opinion that is informed, intelligent, and humane, neither hostile nor patronizing. This is not the place for detail, but there is an admirable statement of the Standing Committee on Migration of the Department of Social Responsibility of the British Council of Churches. This suggests substituting for the negative attitude expressed in: "Keep out as many as we can" something much more positive which might be put in some such form as: "Let us consider our needs and capacity, invite as many entrants as we need and can deal with, then treat them as invited guests." Those who live in areas of immigrant settlement will usually find that there is a Liaison Committee or Friendship Council—the names vary, but in all cases it is an aim to include the widest possible membership. The Committee will provide a focus for public attention on relations between immigrants and the host community, and in a variety of ways will concern itself with housing, education, and employment—all complex subjects not to be summed up in a phrase. Here then is a sphere for practical work. This will not be possible for all— but there is no one who does not help to form a body of opinion in which all are interdependent. Merely by having an opinion you help to influence your Government. And you can, by taking trouble to find out, ensure that your opinion is progressively more positive, less a reaction to fear. It need hardly be pointed out that hostility and humiliation are built up by words and glances; it is not so easy to be sure whether the unkindness is more damaging to its target or to the one who aims the shaft.

5 Overseas Aid and Christian Responsibility[1]

James Mark

Overseas aid is the provision of resources of all kinds by the richer countries of the world to relieve need in the poorer ones and, especially, to help them to overcome their poverty through economic development. The resources may be goods or the money to buy them; they may be the services of specialists and administrators; or they may be skills, transmitted through the training of men and women, either in their own countries or abroad. The aim is to enable the poorer countries to acquire from the richer the ability to create wealth—an ability which these latter have, in historical terms, discovered only recently for themselves. The main effort must be made by the poorer countries themselves, but help from their richer neighbours may be decisive. The process of development through which they must pass involves fundamental changes in their traditional societies and in their outlook on life. The relationships with the richer countries which are created by the provision and acceptance of aid are complex, and may be difficult since it is no easier to receive than to give. The problems—economic, administrative, technical, social, and psychological—are enormous; the issues at stake are no smaller. With the possible exception of the confrontation between Marxist and non-Marxist societies, this is the most important theme in international relations to-day. Both public and private resources are involved. Christians have therefore a responsibility both as individuals who may have something to contribute directly to the effort, and as citizens, in helping to create and to

[1] The views expressed in this article are personal to James Mark. (Ed.)

maintain the public opinion which will support and demand action by governments.

Before we start to consider any general issues it may be as well to mention a few facts which show how aid is developing, both in the private and the public sector. Aid from Government sources is, in quantity, much the more important. Considerably over half of it is given in grants, the rest in loans. The total amount, after deducting the repayments of loans (but not the interest on them), was about $7000 million in 1963, of which nearly $6000 million came from Western countries, rather over $400 million from the Soviet bloc, and about $600 million from international institutions, mainly the International Bank and the International Development Association, which draw the bulk of their funds from Western sources. These figures have risen sharply over the last fifteen years. Between 1950 and 1955 the annual average was not much over $2000 million. Aid from countries outside the Soviet bloc then rose to its present level by 1961, since when it has remained more or less static. Aid from the Soviet bloc has continued to increase, though it is still only a small proportion of the total. Aid from the international agencies has grown a great deal in the last few years, from about $250 million in 1961 to over $600 million in 1963; it was probably even higher last year.

Our own share of the total for 1963 (including our contributions to the international agencies) was rather over $400 million (about £150 million), but it has since increased further. (We normally calculate our aid programme without deducting repayments of capital, so that the figures in Government statements are somewhat higher.) Our official aid programme has risen more gradually and more steadily than that of the Western countries as a whole; it is still increasing, mainly because funds we have already pledged are being spent more quickly. It is now probably about seven per cent of all the aid provided by governments, either directly or indirectly.

Apart from the flow of Government aid the poorer countries can also be helped by private capital from overseas. In some ways this help can often be more effective than Government aid, since capital is closely linked with technical and administrative skill, but private capital expects to earn profits and must go where it can do so. In 1960 and 1961 about $2500 million a year of such capital (after deducting repayments of capital, but not earnings on it) flowed into the poorer countries; the amount then fell significantly, but now seems to have regained the previous level. A good deal of the total is concentrated in particular regions and industries, notably oil.

Information about contributions from private sources is much less adequate, and for this reason the figures are not included in the statistics of aid which are usually quoted. Here again we can say that the amount has increased a good deal in recent years, especially in this country. Most of us recall the World Refugee Year campaign as a kind of breakthrough, which enabled the private organizations working for refugees to raise their annual income from about $£\frac{1}{2}$ million to about $£4$ million. Since then private organizations have continued to make increasing contributions, not only to aid refugees but to combat famine and to help in other aspects of development; the income of Oxfam, for example, rose from $£370,000$ in 1957/8 to $£1,650,000$ in 1961/2, and Christian Aid's income has been over $£1\frac{1}{4}$ million for each of the last two years.

It is important to have a few key figures like these in mind; it is equally important not to be mesmerized by them, since money is by no means an adequate measure of what is provided. Technical assistance (the provision of services and the transfer of skills) costs much less than the provision of goods, but it involves scarce human resources, and it is often a prerequisite to any possibility of capital investment. Private investment is not strictly aid, though it can produce valuable results. Government aid must always be vastly larger in amount than what can be provided from private sources; but how do you compare the value of large transfers of funds raised by the impersonal processes of Government finance with the much smaller contributions of Oxfam and Christian Aid, collected through the devotion and self-sacrifice of individual people? How do you compare the value to the poorer country of the human relationships created by those who go to work there, and the human concern which these express, with the concrete and costly contribution made by a new steel plant? You must use different scales of value. You must recognize that all these forms of help have their place, and that all are interdependent.

The reasons why aid is given are complex, and I shall say more about them later, but one main reason is the fact that the richer countries are increasing their wealth and feel that they must do something to help the poorer to overcome the age-old burden of grinding poverty. The richer countries have passed or are passing through a revolution of a kind hitherto unknown in human history—a revolution which can create affluence. The reasons for this are diverse: the development of science and technology; the emergence of a group of men ready to exploit the possibilities of economic development which are thereby offered; the existence of social and political conditions in which they can make their way; the possibility of accumulating the capital needed for the process of investment which enables economic development to take place. The result is the accumulation of incomparably greater resources behind the individual worker, which naturally enable him or her to produce far more real wealth. This is the "take-off" from an economy in which individuals scratch a bare living, into one in which they can become steadily richer. It is the move into the affluent society. The economies of the poorer countries are expanding also, but since they *are* so much poorer, the increases in absolute terms are much smaller, and the very rapid growth of their population means that there are more mouths to feel. They have inherited the benefits of Western medicine and public health, but their fertility rates have not adapted themselves to the lower death rates. All this is happening in a world which has become much smaller through the revolution in communications. The poorer countries can see what is happening in the richer; they can see, perhaps, what they have to do to share in the increase in wealth and well-being; they can have access to the technology which will create it; but they find it exceedingly difficult to create the conditions necessary to their economic growth. This state of affairs can breed frustration, envy, and resentment.

Can we measure the need, with which this flow of resources is to be matched? Many attempts have been made to do so. The estimate which was used by the poorer countries at the Geneva Conference in 1964 was based on the notion that they were entitled to expect to increase their national incomes by five per cent a year, according to a Resolution of the United Nations; and that they were therefore entitled to the foreign exchange which they needed for this. Their share of world trade and the prices of their exports were falling; so that their foreseeable earnings would leave a gap of about $20,000 million a year by 1970, which would have to be filled by aid and other foreign capital. But whatever the merits of the argument, the estimate took no account of the capacity of the poorer countries to use this amount of money effectively—their lack of plans and administrators, of projects and technicians to run them. Other estimates have therefore put the figure much lower—at perhaps between $12,000 and $15,000 million a year. Even so, it is clearly much more than is being provided at present.

This is a situation which presents great opportunities and equally great dangers. The richer countries have the chance of contributing to the economic betterment of their poorer neighbours in a degree which has never before been possible. They might simply decide that it is their duty to help. This motive has undoubtedly been a strong one; without it, aid, both public and private, would not have grown as it has in the last fifteen years. But aid programmes are the product of a variety of motives; simple moral obligation has not been very effective in isolation. Those nations which have played a small part in international affairs and which have had slight connections with the poorer countries give relatively little aid. Those of the richer countries, like ourselves, which have very close historical connections with individual countries tend to concentrate their aid on them.

It is understandable that a donor country with limited resources should give preference to those countries with which it feels most closely connected, and in which it has perhaps a considerable political and commercial stake. It is equally understandable that an aid programme may be shaped to a considerable extent by political developments, such as the attainment of political independence and the financial settlement which usually accompanies it; this has been true in our own case. But aid may also be used, with varying degrees of subtlety, as a means of exerting political influence. It has been used as a weapon in the cold war. This may be resented by the poorer countries as the exploitation of need for political purposes. For its part a donor country may resent the apparent lack of gratitude which leads the recipient to refuse to conform to its political wishes, and perhaps to criticize its policies. There is, further, the complication introduced by commercial motives. Trade may in the past have followed the flag; to-day it certainly follows aid, since a great deal of aid is "tied" (in the current jargon) to the financing of goods and services from the country providing it. There may be good reasons for this; the country providing the aid may fear the effects on its balance of payments if it provided aid which can be spent in other countries. More positively, exporters not unnaturally look to aid as a means of financing orders from the poorer countries. They may well provide goods which are needed, but to allow commercial motives to influence aid policy can lead to a confusion of motives and policies. It may arouse resentment in the poorer country, which may feel that it is not getting what it wants, and is expected to pay dearly for it and to be grateful into the bargain.

Finally, the country providing aid may come to feel, after a time, that there is simply no end to the process. Sacrifices have to be made to provide the aid; this goes on year after year; the visible results seem disappointing, quite apart from the lack of gratitude; and the taxpayer begins to wonder whether he is not merely pouring away money which might have been used to better purpose at home. There is some evidence that feelings of this sort have developed recently in several of the richer countries; they may be reflected in the failure of aid programmes generally to rise much further after the rapid climb during the late 1950s.

On their side the poorer countries have the opportunity, which they had been unable to create for themselves, of overcoming their poverty. This is a challenge to co-operation with the richer countries, and to dedicated and constructive effort at home. Rapid economic development itself has its less attractive sides—the cult of material advance, the emergence of the thruster, the sacrifice of inherited values and the failure to replace them. These aspects, however, real though they are, are somewhat outside the scope of the present essay, where I am concerned only with the effects on relations between donor and recipient. The position of the recipient is not easy. He may feel that he must escape from it by asserting that he has a right to the transfer of resources (I will not say to aid) from the richer countries; and that he should have these in the form of earnings from trade, rather than as aid, since he will thereby escape the feeling of receiving charity and be freer to use the money as he wishes. This was the argument of the poorer countries at the Geneva Conference.

It is not so long ago that the Colonies were regarded as faraway places which supported themselves. Richer and poorer countries have now been thrown together in a closer relationship than ever before, with the sharing of wealth as a dominant preoccupation. These closer relations can be for good or ill. We can achieve a new spirit of international cooperation or, on the one hand, resentful disillusionment, and on the other, envious frustration.

What is the responsibility of Christians in this situation? To a large extent it is no different from that of anyone else. They may see it in terms different from non-Christians, and they may, for example, remember the words of 1 John 3. 17:

E

Whoso hath this world's good, and seeth his brother hath need, and shutteth up his bowels of compassion from him, how dwelleth the love of God in him?

Non-Christians would think, rather, in terms of the obligations of human beings to each other—of the fellowship of our common humanity. There is, moreover, a distinctive Christian perspective in which these problems must be seen. Man does not live by bread alone, and material advancement is not the ultimate end of life. But it is not for those who have bread to say this to those who have none. In practice, Christians have much the same responsibility as non-Christians.

The first necessity is obviously that we should feel a concern for the situation: the compassion which makes us realize that we must do something about it. This, if it is defined widely enough, may say all that needs to be said, but compassion can easily be interpreted in sentimental terms. We need understanding also—understanding of the difficulties of the poorer countries and of the feelings to which the situation gives rise in them. Compassion does not necessarily mean always giving way to every demand that the poorer countries may make; some of these may need to be firmly but sympathetically resisted. We need understanding, equally, of the mixture of motives in our own countries, which have led to the giving of aid; we need to distinguish aid and the sacrifice which it must entail from the service, however justifiable, of our own interests, political or commercial. We need a kind of open-minded empiricism in approaching the problem. There is, for example, no "just price" for the commodities which the poorer countries have to sell, and no share in world trade to which they are entitled as of right. On the other hand, we cannot ignore the effects on their well-being and on their prospects of development if these turn against them. We must recognize the problem, though the finding of solutions demands not merely this awareness but a good deal both of technical, economic, and also political expertise. We need intelligent generosity. The will to give is, by itself, not enough. Finally, we need patience and stamina for the long haul; a readiness to accept that the co-operative effort which is needed will extend over a long time; that there will be mistakes and set-backs; that our generosity may often seem not to be appreciated, and our motives misunderstood. We shall need not to weary in well-doing, nor must we proclaim either to ourselves or to those who benefit from our generosity that it *is* well-doing. (On the other hand, Christians in the countries receiving aid should show, and encourage others to show, a friendly appreciation of the help offered them, even when clumsily offered.) All this will affect individual Christians, like others, in different ways. All of us can give to the private agencies which undertake work in the poorer countries. Some can help in the work of collecting. All of us can help, as individuals, to make sure that the issue is kept before public opinion and not submerged in the clamant needs which compete for public funds and private generosity. Some will be able to offer their help, either as experts, or under the schemes for Voluntary Service Overseas. It is for each of us to ask what is his duty in this situation.

6 Defence and Disarmament

Anthony Buzzard

This chapter covers the problem of what to do with military power. It does not include the important question of peaceful settlement of disputes or peaceful adjustment to change.

Section 1 considers the Christian criteria specifically concerned with the use of force. Section 2 summarizes the relevant world situation and outlook to-day. Section 3 suggests possible policies and steps which Christians might support after applying their Christian criteria to to-day's situation.

1. CHRISTIAN CRITERIA

It will have been gathered from the Bishop of Leicester's article that man is the peak of God's creation; that Christ pinpointed love as the foundation of all man-to-man relationships; and that Christians must therefore respect creation and the life of man in a spirit of love. Equally, however, it has been made clear that since Christians are involved in human history, they must also respect the power of the State and other human organizations when they are compatible with human life, love, and a just world order; but that when they are *not*, Christians must renounce the "world" and its organizations. Whether or not *any* killing can be compatible with the above has divided Christians for centuries.

PACIFISM

Some pacifists believe, as a matter of principle, that this cannot be so in the light of our Lord's injunctions to love your enemy and to turn the other cheek, and of his refusal to allow his disciples to defend him by force when faced with the cross. Other pacifists judge that as a calculation of consequences readiness to fight encourages more wars than it prevents, breeds fear and hate, and that the money spent in preparing for war would be better spent in removing its causes.

NON-PACIFISM

Non-pacifist Christians believe that readiness to fight can often prevent war, and that if it fails it can sometimes be the lesser evil. Fighting may, therefore, be a duty to one's neighbours, as it is sometimes for policemen. Though the Sermon on the Mount's ethic of love is already applicable to such human relationships as happy family life, non-pacifists recognize that it can, at present, be applied only indirectly, through the medium of law and justice, to international societies, in which Christians form but a small minority.

The Thirty-seventh Article of Religion is sometimes quoted in support of non-pacifism, but it is doubtful whether we should surrender an individual conscience to national authority as completely as was assumed when those Articles were written in 1562.

NON-PACIFIST DOCTRINE AND
INTERNATIONAL LAW

Many attempts to define the degree to which fighting is justified have been made since St Augustine began to develop the "just war" doctrine in the fourth century, and out of these grew international law, culminating in the United Nations Charter. Though some of these were wrongly conceived, many have been ignored or abused, and some may now be out of date, they contain certain general criteria which seem impossible to deny morally, though there is plenty of scope for legalistic argument.

Briefly, these criteria indicate that peace and justice for all is the aim, and that resort to force can be justified only in defence of the common interest, as a last resort, as the lesser evil, and when there is a reasonable prospect of victory for justice—not necessarily victory for one side. The basic principle is that of *proportion*, i.e. there must be good prospects of the evil resulting from resisting an aggressor remaining *proportionate* to the good expected to be gained by doing so.

Once at war, aims in war—war aims—must be similarly restricted. They must be purely defensive, designed to stop the aggressor's physical attack, and not used as an instrument of any other national or international policy. "Unconditional surrender" is hardly consistent with such aims. Rather must there be a return to negotiations at the earliest moment compatible with overall justice.

Means in war, too, must be kept proportionate to the issue at stake and to these aims. But they must also be reasonably *discriminating* and under *control* of the human conscience. Intentional attacks against neutrals or non-combatants (those not directly participating) are basically wrong. Wrong, too, are indiscriminate attacks against military targets which injure neutrals or non-combatants unintentionally to a degree which is disproportionate to the just military advantage to be gained. So too are uncontrolled means likely to lead to these.

The right of *reprisals* provides the only possible exception to these limitations in means. But reprisals are justified only to the extent necessary to cause an enemy to desist from violating these limitations, i.e. in so far as good may be achieved. Reprisals taken beyond this point, if he should fail to desist, or for revenge, or in any way in which more harm than good is done, cannot be justified. Here again the principle of proportion applies.

There is some disagreement as to whether the basic wrong of intentional attack on non-combatants can be justified by way of reprisal for similar enemy action, but it is clear that that is the only conceivable justification for such action.

Finally war must be stopped, if necessary, to comply with these limitations.

If God gave man any right at all to kill in defence of man, then twin-born with that right was the responsibility to ensure that he does so with due respect for proportion, discrimination, control, and strictly limited reprisals. In other words, we must work on the same principle as we would expect from a policeman or from the international police force which we cannot yet organize.

NUCLEAR PACIFISM

Some Christians consider that these traditional principles lose all relevance when applied to nuclear weapons, and must be rejected in this respect as a matter of principle. They feel that, in their power and poisonous effects, nuclear weapons are so destructive of life and creativity that even non-pacifist Christians must say "No" to any use of them in any circumstances. And since *possession* of them implies intention to *use* them if necessary, Britain should have nothing to do with any alliances which rely on even the possession of nuclear weapons. This "unilateralism" as a matter of principle is sometimes called "nuclear pacifism".

Other Christians, however, feel that there could be a moral distinction between possessing and using nuclear weapons, and perhaps between different types of nuclear weapons and the targets against which they might be used. They also warn against salving our own personal consciences in preference to solving the problems threatening humanity. They therefore feel that it is their duty to reserve judgement on the issue until after the world situation has been reviewed and the consequences of unilateralism can be calculated.

2. PRESENT SITUATION AND PROSPECTS

THE THREAT TO PEACE AND JUSTICE

The balance of crisis has now moved—at least temporarily—from Europe to the peripheral areas of Asia, Africa, and Latin America, where racial and colonial problems, the rising power of China, the problems of the under-developed countries and the East/West rivalry for influence over them are now more likely to cause breaches of the peace.

Nevertheless, the central front of Europe, with its un-resolved German problem, remains the main bone of con-tention and the greatest military confrontation between the two great Powers. If Russian interests were under heavy pressure elsewhere in the world, she would be sorely tempted to apply pressure to Berlin or its corridors, where she holds the West to ransom. Central Europe remains, therefore, the most likely, if not the only, area in which war could escalate unintentionally to the thermo-nuclear proportions which nobody wants.

Meanwhile the principal basic threat to justice and peace lies in the Russian and Chinese determination to spread their influence and ideology by, apparently, any means which pay. These at the moment are undoubtedly mainly at the subversion and insurgency level. But we do not know whether pressure would be raised to the conventional or nuclear levels if the West relaxed its defence. There also seem to be lesser basic threats of aggression from the present régimes of Egypt, Indonesia, and North Vietnam. This is not to say that the West is free from blame, or that some of this apparent aggressiveness is not due to our unduly rigid, anti-communist, and imperialistic attitude. It is possible that *some* of the aggressiveness may be due to our measures of defence appearing aggressive to our adversaries.

WESTERN DISSENSIONS

Unfortunately there is much Western disagreement as to the intention of Russia, China, their satellites, and the more aggressive smaller Powers; and therefore on the way in which they should be handled. American refusal to recognize China, West Germany's fear of recognizing East Germany, French desire for independence of America, and Britain's uncertainty of her future rôle, all obstruct agreement on defence and disarmament problems—particularly the control of nuclear weapons and how to prevent their proliferation.

This problem remains unsolved, with Multi-Lateral Force (MLF) now largely discredited, the Atlantic Nuclear Force (ANF) hanging fire, but with America proposing closer four or five Power nuclear planning within the North Atlantic Treaty Organization (NATO). Meanwhile, with China's bomb about to threaten India, the problem of guaranteeing countries outside the North Atlantic Treaty Organization from nuclear blackmail is becoming urgent, if anti-proliferation agreements are to be secured.

Interdependence in the sharing of conventional commitments and the procurement of conventional arms is also lacking throughout the West and becoming urgent in the face of the ever-rising cost of arms.

UNITED NATIONS DISSENSIONS

Progress in the development of the United Nations peace-keeping machinery, so important for both peace and disarmament, is obstructed by the disagreement on financing it. This is due to disagreement on how the peace-keeping forces shall be controlled—by the Security Council or by the Assembly. This, in turn, reflects a basic Western fear that the peace-keeping force will too often continue to be vetoed, and a Russian fear that a two-thirds majority will too often be used against her interests.

There is also the problem of getting Communist China into the United Nations and of *her* veto, once she is there.

Until, therefore, Western and Communist interests and ideas of justice come closer, there seems little hope for many years of more than occasional and limited reliance on the United Nations for prompt peace-keeping action.

THE BALANCE OF POWER

At the conventional level of fighting, which is the only level at which fighting is likely to start—as a result of some local dispute, insurgency, aggression, accident, or miscalculation —both the Russians and Chinese enjoy considerable superiority over the West. This is not because they have any great *overall* superiority in conventional strength, but because geography favours them with short, internal land lines of communication, which enable them to strike outwards in any direction round the Iron Curtain (from Northern

Scandinavia to Korea) much more quickly than we can reinforce any of these areas with our much longer and slower,
external sea and air lines of communication. Because of their
closed societies they can also move more secretly than we can,
and, if potential aggressors, would have the initiative. Even
if we were potential aggressors, geography would make it
extremely difficult for us to make a successful conventional
attack across the Iron Curtain.

On the other hand, at the strategic nuclear level, the West
—particularly America—enjoys great superiority over the
Russians and of course over the Chinese, not only owing to
our larger number of nuclear weapons, but also because
geography here favours us. For the Americans are able to
launch their missiles and bombers from land and sea bases
about three times as close to Russian and Chinese vitals as
Russian and Chinese bases (except for some submarines) can
be to American vitals.

This asymetrical situation is bad for peace and disarmament for the following reasons. First, our inferiority in conventional capability may cause us to threaten and perhaps
use tactical atomic weapons *first*, which is morally repugnant,
unstable, and liable to lead to escalation and uncontrolled,
indiscriminate, and disproportionate war.

Secondly, the more we rely on the first use of tactical
atomic weapons the more temptation there is for individual
Western countries to demand independent control of nuclear
weapons, for fear that their allies will not initiate nuclear
war in their defence. This, of course, encourages proliferation.

Thirdly, our over-threatening of Russia and China at the
nuclear level, and their over-threatening of us at the conventional level, maintains tension and distrust, makes
balanced reductions of arms difficult, and so obstructs disarmament.

DISARMAMENT NEGOTIATIONS

This, and because there has not yet been the necessary
political relaxation, is why no progress has yet been made

with either the Western or Russian plans for general and
comprehensive disarmament.

Some partial or "collateral" measures have, however,
been achieved—cessation of tests other than those underground, the hot line between Washington and Moscow, and
an unverified agreement not to orbit nuclear weapons in
space. Underground test bans, anti-proliferation agreements,
arms reductions in Central Europe, measures against surprise attack, "bomber bonfires", "nuclear freezes", cut-offs
in nuclear production, and reductions to "minimum deterrents" have all been proposed, but as yet all are opposed
by certain countries who might become relatively worse off.
And Russia seems particularly loath to accept verification
of *remaining*—as opposed to discarded—arms, especially in
her own country, possibly because of the secrecy advantage
which her closed society gives her.

There is, in fact, too much concern all round for the
national interest, and not enough for the common interest.
It is also possible that the Russian leaders still look on disarmament as a means of furthering their political and ideo-
logical aims.

TIME FACTOR

Meanwhile time is not on our side, with the rising power
of China, with the gap between the "have" and "have not"
countries widening, with more and more countries becoming
able to make and afford nuclear weapons, and with the cost
of conventional weapons always increasing. But fortunately
defensive weapons are gaining power over offensive weapons
at the conventional level. And the fear of nuclear war does
seem to inspire caution.

3. DECISION AND ACTION

In deciding what general defence policy to support in the
face of this situation, we cannot avoid the evidence that both
Russia and China have committed acts of conventional
aggression since the Second World War (as indeed the West

has, too); that it may therefore well be our duty to deter
them from doing so again (and their duty to deter us); that
they face us with superior conventional capability; and that
our threat to use tactical atomic weapons first, together with
our *possession* of thermo-nuclear weapons, may well have
deterred them from further aggressions with their superior
conventional capability. This is the cruel dilemma facing
Christians in the West to-day.

MASSIVE RETALIATION

One possible attitude is to exploit to the maximum the deterrent effect of our thermo-nuclear superiority and of our
threat to use tactical atomic weapons first, in the hope that
the West will thus prevent *all* war, or at least all except the
smallest wars. Such a policy recommends only the minimum
of conventional defence and the minimum of control over
escalation, so that our adversaries may see the risks of em-
barking on any war. This is certainly the cheapest policy
financially. But it is discarded by most Christians as incompatible with the Christian criteria of proportion, discrimination, and control, unless one decides upon a complete policy
of bluff, which could not surely last. It is also incompatible
with the standards on which we are trying to develop the
United Nations peace-keeping and police forces. Nor would
it lead to arms control or disarmament. Indeed, as we have
seen, it encourages proliferation. Moreover as a deterrent it
is liable to prove too "horrific" to be credible in a crisis and
too great a gamble in a world where conflicts are liable to
arise as a result of miscalculation or misunderstanding. For
these reasons massive retaliation has now become largely
discredited in the West, except in France and in some German circles.

UNILATERALISM

At the other extreme lies the policy of unilateralism, which
calculates that a less dangerous way out of our dilemma is
for Britain to decline to have anything to do with nuclear
weapons and to opt out of the North Atlantic Treaty Organi-

zation (NATO), the Central Treaty Organization (CENTO), and the South East Asia Treaty Organization (SEATO), if necessary to achieve this. It envisages using our remaining conventional strength on behalf of the United Nations or for other legitimate purposes, but independently of the Western Alliances, particularly America. And it claims that disarmament and the development of the United Nations peace-keeping machinery could then be pursued more successfully in conjunction with the uncommitted countries. Its proponents believe that the admitted risks involved in this policy are less than those involved in any alternative.

GRADUALISM

Between these policies of massive retaliation and unilateralism lies that of gradualism, which holds that the removal of Britain's influence, conventional forces, and overseas bases from all Western Alliances would increase Western conventional inferiority to such a degree as to make nuclear war and proliferation more likely. Nor do gradualists feel that an uncommitted Britain could solve the problems of disarmament and the control of the United Nations peace-keeping machinery any better than at present. Instead they feel that better prospects lie in Britain's remaining in the Western Alliances and using her influence to modify Western policies on the following lines.

CRISIS POLICY

They believe that the lesser evil at the moment is to accept Western *possession* of nuclear weapons, at least so long as potential aggressors possess them, because the deterrent effect of this seems to be in the interests of humanity. Indeed it might be morally irresponsible to put the Russian and Chinese leaders in the position of nuclear monopoly which we could not resist exploiting at Hiroshima and Nagasaki. Nor do we wish to make possible again prolonged and world-wide conventional wars.

But at the same time gradualists demand that if deterrence should fail—as it might—then nuclear weapons should be used, if at all, only within the limitations of proportion, discrimination, control, and strictly limited reprisals discussed in Section 1, and indeed conventional weapons must be thus restrained too. We must rely as little as possible on the first use of tactical atomic weapons; we must exercise all possible control of them and of other weapons; we must observe proper discrimination between armed forces and non-combatants, and we must certainly never resort to general nuclear bombardment of cities. If necessary, we must cease fire to conform to these limitations, regardless of what the enemy may be doing to us.

Gradualists do not demand, however, that their governments should announce in advance precisely in what circumstances or in what way they would or would not use nuclear and other weapons, for that is liable to reduce deterrence and bring on the nuclear war which it must be the first responsibility of all Christians to prevent.

In other words gradualists accept a limited, responsible use of military power and its deterrent effect on the same basis —no more and no less—as that which we would expect of the international police force which is not yet in being. One would hardly expect such a force to maintain world order in the face of national nuclear weapons without itself possessing them.

PLANNING POLICY

At the same time gradualists insist too that this situation be considered as transitory only, and that vigorous efforts be made to move to one in which nuclear and other arms are brought under international control, reduced, and finally abolished, except for those which may have to be left in the hands of a world police force. They recognize, however, that this is likely to take a long time and that it must be tackled step by step in parallel with political and economic measures to reduce tension, distrust, and frustration.

Defence policies must be planned so that they assist arms control, disarmament, and the development of the United Nations peace-keeping machinery. At the same time arms control and disarmament policies must be planned so that they make defence sense. And high priority must be given in both defence and disarmament planning to improving our ability to implement the restrained crisis policy described above. First and foremost in this must be our ability to control any fighting so that it does not escalate unintentionally into the nuclear war which nobody wants.

ANTI-PROLIFERATION MEASURES

To assist this, and to prevent the present arms situation from becoming any worse, one prime objective must clearly be to bring existing independent nuclear deterrents under centralized international control, and to discourage their spread to other countries. Clearly this was the general motive behind Britain's Atlantic Nuclear Force proposal, which was also a healthy admission that individual countries—never reliable judges in their own cause—should not act independently, at least at the thermo-nuclear level of fighting which affects all.

Some such nuclear sharing within the West, combined with some Western guarantee to uncommitted countries against nuclear blackmail, should greatly encourage nuclear Powers to sign non-dissemination agreements and non-nuclear Powers to sign non-acquisition agreements. This, together with an agreement to cease underground testing and to freeze or reduce nuclear means of delivery, should improve the prospects of checking proliferation.

REDUCING THE ASYMMETERY OF THE EAST/WEST BALANCE

A second and equally important objective is to remove from the East/West balance of power some of the present asymmetry which—as described earlier—encourages escalation, proliferation, and the tension and distrust which obstructs disarmament. As an important part of this, we must reduce to a minimum our reliance upon the first use of tactical atomic weapons, which arises from our conventional inferiority.

ARMS LIMITATION AGREEMENTS
IN EUROPE

The most effective move would be to persuade Russia to surrender some of her conventional superiority in exchange for our—particularly America's—surrender of some nuclear superiority. And central Europe is the most important area in which to start, because this is where we rely most upon the first use of tactical atomic weapons, where the issues are so vital and explosive, and where relaxation is needed so badly to help solve the Berlin and German problems. Moreover the Rapacki and Gomulka proposals, together with Mr Khruschev's offer of observation posts against surprise attack in Central Europe, suggest that Russia might well accept some arms limitation agreement here.

Since Russia's conventional superiority in Central Europe arises from her ability to reinforce her present twenty-two divisions there very much more quickly and heavily than we can ours, we might suggest a balanced limitation of offensive conventional forces (for example tanks) on both sides around the present strength. At the same time we might suggest a balanced withdrawal of some of the larger and more inspectable tactical atomic means of delivery (for example fighter bombers and light bombers) on both sides, combined with a unilateral offer to keep our polaris submarines out of the Mediterranean, or to destroy more of our bombers in the proposed "bomber bonfire" agreement than those destroyed by Russia.

The main objection to such a proposal would probably come from Germany, on the grounds that it would discriminate against her. But by seeking similar agreements on the northern and southern flanks of Europe, we might convince her that it is necessary because of her geography—not because of her history.

ARMS LIMITATION AGREEMENTS WITH CHINA

With the confrontation with Russia thus eased and stabilized and the balance of power *vis-à-vis* Russia more symmetrical, Part 1 of the Russian and Western plans for general and comprehensive disarmament would become a little less hopeless. At the same time some Western—and Russian—conventional strength would be freed to help balance the growing strength of China. This would reduce our reliance upon the first use of tactical atomic weapons against *her* too.

This in turn should enable America to relax her nuclear threats against China, and help her to bring the latter into the United Nations, so that in due course we might negotiate arms limitation agreements with her in South-East Asia and other areas of confrontation, on lines similar to that operating in Korea for the last ten years.

WESTERN CONVENTIONAL INTERDEPENDENCE AND SHARING OF COMMITMENTS

The easing of the confrontation with Russia might also encourage European countries to assist America and Britain in maintaining law and order outside Europe when the United Nations is unable to act. Not only would such issues then be more likely to be handled with justice and impartiality, but the accusation of American and British "imperialism", perhaps sometimes justified, would begin to lose credence. Moreover, with Europe thus becoming more outward-looking, Britain's political entry into Europe might become more practicable.

Much needed saving in men and arms would also result, with correspondingly greater resources becoming available to aid the developing countries and to help remove the causes of unrest. Thus, too, the West might better implement the United Nations principle of collective security when the United Nations is unable to operate itself, and at the same time set the best possible example for its development, without which general and comprehensive disarmament will never be possible.

CONCLUSION

As an alternative to the extremes of massive retaliation and unilateralism, gradualism thus offers a policy which demands

F

that crises be handled with proper proportion, discrimination and control; and that Western defence and disarmament planning be so pursued as both to improve our ability so to handle crises, and to help us towards relaxation, disarmament, and the development of the United Nations peace-keeping.

And as first steps in this planning policy gradualists envisage anti-proliferation measures, reduction of the asymmetry of the East/West balance by seeking arms limitation agreements in Europe (followed later by similar agreements with China), and better Western conventional interdependence and the sharing of commitments outside Europe.

Though this policy of gradualism falls short of the demands of unilateralists, pacifists, and nuclear pacifists, some of these may be prepared to support it as a step towards their more ambitious aims. Others, however, may feel that their Christian witness requires them to support only the policy of their choice. But all Christians must surely study, pray, and act on these baffling defence and disarmament problems and never cease trying to reconcile their views with those who differ from them.

Thus, and with God's grace, we may find the unity and common mind with which to pursue his will for the preservation of human life, love, and a just world order.

7 Man's Dominion

Hugh Montefiore

Man has dominion over all nature. This clear teaching of the Bible has been endorsed by centuries of Christian tradition. According to the first chapter of Genesis, God created man and woman in the image of God, and gave them rule and authority over all that was in the world:

> And God blessed them, and God said unto them, Be fruitful and multiply, and replenish the earth and subdue it: and have dominion over the fish of the sea and over the fowl of the air, and over every living thing that moveth upon the earth.

The passage presupposes the creation of Adam and Eve as the first man and woman, but man's dominion does not itself depend on the literal truth of this ancient myth. It is inherent in humanity as such. Yet it is not an arbitrary endowment. It is given to man because he is made "in the image of God". Whatever else this enigmatic phrase may mean, it includes two of man's qualities or endowments which distinguish him from the beasts: the gift of intelligence and the sense of responsibility. It follows therefore that unless man exercises his dominion over nature with intelligence and with a proper sense of responsibility, he is failing to use God's gifts as they were intended to be used. Gross abuse will inevitably lead to judgement and wrath.

This passage in Gen. 1 does not stand alone. The same viewpoint is expressed by the author of Ps. 8. The *Revised Standard Version* brings out the meaning best:

> When I look at thy heavens, the work of thy fingers,
> The moon and the stars which thou hast established;
> What is man that thou art mindful of him,
> Or the son of man that thou dost care for him?

Yet thou hast made him little less than God,
And dost crown him with glory and honour.
Thou hast given him dominion over the works of thy hands,
Thou hast put all things under his feet.

There is literally nothing that lies outside man's ability to control and order. As the author of the Epistle to the Hebrews writes, "Now, in putting everything in subjection to man, God left nothing outside his control." When those words were written, man's control was potential rather than actual: to-day, nearly two thousand years later, it has been vastly extended, and it is not difficult to imagine the time when it will be complete. These powers have been given to man because he has been created "a little less than God". He acts, as it were, as God's vicegerent. He must therefore exercise these powers in accordance with God's moral nature. His sense of responsibility, as well as his status in creation, must be little less than God's.

What does it mean to behave responsibly towards creation? The first question to be asked is whether man has a prime duty to conserve all species which have evolved and which still exist on land, in the air, or in the oceans. It may well be that the destruction of lower forms of life may be detrimental to man; but the point here is rather different. Has man a duty to preserve species for his own sake? Wanton destruction for the mere pleasure of hunting (a fate that has almost eliminated gazelles in Jordan) or wanton cruelty to animals (the subject of prosecutions by the Royal Society for the Prevention of Cruelty to Animals) shows a contempt for God's creation and is not to be tolerated. But if certain wild animals can only live in uncultivated areas, and if those areas are needed for cultivation, should man have any scruples in clearing them? If animals eat food which man needs for himself, should he hesitate to destroy them, even if this may result in the elimination of a whole species? Does man owe a living to beasts and birds and fish for their own sake? It is hard to see on what grounds this could be established. It is important here not to confuse sentiment with morality. Children like playing with a Noah's Ark, and many adults are ornithologists and nature-lovers. There is much to admire in the wonderful variety of species that have evolved, and no doubt many of them can be preserved somewhere or other in National Parks. But man is made in the image of God, and the beasts are not. They must give way before the needs of man. If the Africans eliminate the hippopotamus by clearing the jungle, it may be regrettable, but it is not immoral. After all, nobody minds that wolves have been eliminated from this country, and many farmers wish that all foxes and rabbits could suffer the same fate. Species inevitably evolve and decline. No one, for example, thinks that the disappearance of the brontosaurus is a disaster.

Man therefore has a right to destroy animals, birds, and fish, not wantonly or cruelly but in accordance with his needs. The same principles apply to animal production. The combination of demand and competition makes it inevitable that the agricultural industry will develop into industrial agriculture. Factory farms will increase. The points to watch concern the nutritive value of meat produced, the possible danger to humanity from the drugs given to the animals, and the frontiers of cruelty. The last named particularly need definition. Is it or is it not cruel to rear a calf so that it cannot turn round or see daylight? This is a moral question, as yet unanswered.

Man has dominion not only over the beasts, but also over the inorganic resources of the world: minerals, metals, rocks, coal, gas, and petroleum deposits. There was a time when these resources seemed limitless, but at the present rate of development they will not last much longer. Already supplies of gold are more difficult to obtain. No metal is in indefinite supply. It is said that the coal reserves of Europe will last only another half century. Has man the moral right to use the raw materials of the earth without reference to succeeding generations?

Such a question is seldom asked: it produces moral discomfort. And yet it must be faced sometime, together with the issues that it raises. A distinction may be made, perhaps, between metals and minerals in general, and those raw materials which are capable of being used as sources of power. For, after all, metals that have been mined and used may be used again. Scrap iron is used for the production of modern steel, and there is no reason, in principle, why other metals should not increasingly be used second-hand. None of the raw materials in the earth will suffice for man's continued use until this planet can no longer support life, when in the distant future the sun expands into a "red giant". We can hardly ration ourselves to a certain quota of minerals in each generation in order to conserve unknown reserves for an unknown future. In any case we cannot guess future conditions. It may be possible, in thirty or forty centuries' time, or much sooner, to import minerals and metals from other planets or stars. It may be possible to manufacture metals or efficient substitutes.

Man is therefore justified in using raw materials, but this can degenerate into abuse. The mineral wealth of the world has been slowly formed over countless millennia and we shall have squandered most of it in the reckless extravaganza of a few centuries. *And we cannot stop!* This is not a matter for personal decision and for personal ethics. It concerns national and international policies. The economies of all countries are geared to increased production, whether they are planned on capitalist or socialist lines. The greater the production, the cheaper the cost; and the cheaper the cost, the easier it is—provided there is a demand for the finished product—to overcome competition in the home market (in capitalist countries) and, for both socialist and capitalist countries, to win sales in the overseas market. This system works for the benefit of all, in the sense that more and more people are able to afford and to enjoy more products at cheaper prices. The result is a general rise in the standard of living, which is universally agreed to be desirable. In socialist countries industries are usually large because they are State-owned; and in capitalist countries larger and larger groups are tending to emerge, precisely because it is cheaper to rationalize industry by mass production. Expansion is necessary for all types of economy. Any one country which decided to restrict production, for whatever reason, would be likely to suffer. A country would suffer particularly badly if, like our own, it cannot produce enough food for its own inhabitants, but has to pay for imported foodstuffs from the profit that it makes on its exported products. Any workable plan for restricting production would have to be world-wide to stand a chance of being effective. Yet to-day, far from advancing towards world-government, the United Nations Organization itself is in jeopardy. Yet, even if we cannot arrest increased production at will, we ought to know the effect of the process on posterity.

Some raw materials are irreplaceable because we convert them into power. Already, in America and in Europe people's lives have been transformed by the use of cheap power for industry, locomotion, and home use. The traditional sources of power have been coal, gas, and petroleum. Yet the coal-fields of the world are unlikely to continue production more than a century or two.[1] Large supplies of natural gas are still being found, such as those which are at present being exploited for European use from beneath the Sahara desert.[2] Pessimists have frequently predicted the exhaustion of the earth's petroleum deposits, but new finds are continually being made, and great sums are expended in searching for them (for example, in the North Sea). Yet, although the reserves are large, consumption, unless checked, is likely to rise, for petrol is cheap to produce and easy to convert into power. It is hard to believe that, at the present growth rate of production, the natural supplies of petrol will last for more than another century or two.[3] And yet this explosive

[1] The proved reserves of coal will last for 290 years at the present rate of production. Most of these reserves are in China or America.

[2] The proved reserves of gas will last for sixteen years at the present rate of production.

[3] The proved reserves of liquid fuel will last for thirty years at the present rate of production. It has been calculated that five to ten times the present proved reserves may be recoverable from conventional deposits of oil and gas, in addition to which there are tar sand and oil shale deposits.

liquid took millions of years to form beneath the surface of the earth.

Since 1950 the world consumption of primary energy has been increasing at five per cent compound per annum. The same growth laws probably apply to energy consumption as to national growth. It might be said that necessity is the mother of invention, and that further sources of energy will soon be opened up for man. Possibly there is a future in the fuel cell or Magneto-Hydro-Dynamics. Already power from nuclear reactors is competitive in price with power derived from conventional sources. Are we not justified in using up conventional sources of power at our good pleasure, confident that future generations will have far more abundant and cheaper sources?

At first sight the answer might seem to be Yes. But there are limits to the harnessing of the sun's rays or the force of gravity. More important, there are atomic reactors. These will probably produce cheap power, but they will also produce atomic waste. The degree of contamination caused by the explosion of nuclear devices is disturbing enough already. Already men and women are dying from the effects of radiation, and this will continue. It has been calculated that it will be thirty or forty years before all the radioactive dust, hurled into the stratosphere as the result of atomic explosions, will settle again upon earth. But the problems of nuclear waste are even more pressing. The world is now in 1965 probably producing about fifty tons of nuclear waste per year. All countries want to build reactors, and those who have them are expanding their plants. The waste is bound to increase, but there is as yet no way of reducing the exceedingly long life of these decaying substances. The radioactive life of the waste is greater than that of its containers. Furthermore water which is used for cooling purposes, although it is purified, is still slightly radioactive, and this radioactivity gradually builds up. If it is stored in caverns, it tends to contaminate ground water.

Thus, to squander the conventional sources of power and so to force posterity to rely on nuclear power is to put the

future at hazard. No doubt there is always risk in all under-
takings, and we may be content to assume that posterity will
find the answer to the problems of nuclear waste. But can
we be sure? May the answer be found too late? It is a risk
we have to weigh.

There are other forms of poison as well as nuclear contamination. The use of pesticides can be exceedingly dangerous to posterity. It is indisputable that some pesticides
are necessary, especially if the food resources of the world
are to be adequate for an increasing population. A few years
ago the Food and Agricultural Organization of the United
Nations Organization gave the annual loss through pests in
bread, cereals, and rice alone as 33 million tons, sufficient to
feed some 150 million people. It is natural and proper that
the resources of modern science should be mobilized in an
attempt to reduce these and similar losses. This would not
only add to the farmers' profits, but it also would make more
food available to a world where already thousands are
starving.

The long-term effects of pesticides are not generally appreciated. In the first place, the poison may kill off the birds
and other animals which are the natural enemies of pests,
while the pests themselves tend to become immunized
against the poison, so that stronger and stronger measures
are necessary to keep the pests at bay. (The immunization of
bacteria against modern powerful antibiotics is not dissimilar.) Thus the last state of the land may be worse than the
first. Secondly, some pesticides poison the soil itself, which
may become less productive. These pesticides, improperly
handled, can kill those who handle them, while the poison
is washed down rivers into the sea, contaminating fish and
birds alike. (For example, in 1964 over 5 million fish, duck,
and other birds died in the Mississippi basin as a result of
drainage from crops sprayed with insecticides.) Thirdly, and
most important, some pesticides are potentially dangerous to
man. As a result of predation, traces of poisonous pesticides
can build up in birds and animals, and finally man himself
can be endangered by the meat, game, fish, and vegetables

which he consumes. Worse still, the hazards can be handed on to the next generation. The poison tends to be stored in the subcutaneous fat, and does not all pass through the body; and it may be passed on to future generations both by breast milk and through the process of reproduction. Genetic changes can take place, and human posterity may be put at hazard.

Poisons which nature produces in minimal doses have been sprayed in thousands of tons upon the earth in the hope of greater gains and higher profits. These powerful pesticides have not yet been used many years, but already the effects of their use can be seen in the most unlikely places (for example, traces have been found in penguins in the Antarctic and even in rainwater). What will happen if their use continues on the present scale, no one really knows. There is a real danger that humanity, in search of more and cheaper food here and now, may be entailing poison, and consequent sickness, upon posterity. The most potentially dangerous of these chemical sprays are chlorinated hydrocarbons, mostly in the D.D.T. group. Many of them may be freely bought in retail shops for use in back gardens.

There are, at the moment, no international agencies engaged in research on the effect of these toxic sprays, and, of course, no international agency exists which could possibly enforce the prohibition or curtailment of their use. Each country does what is right in its own eyes. Thus for some years the use of dieldrin for sheep dip has been forbidden in New Zealand, but it is only two years since Great Britain followed suit, and then only because bird-lovers were concerned because of the virtual extinction of rare birds of prey due to its poisonous residues. When the restriction was announced, the Shell International Chemical Company issued a public statement to the effect that this prohibition was unjustified and against the public interest!

Whatever we may think of this country, it is plain that there are powerful business interests at stake. In some countries private interest may be strong enough to influence public policy—to the detriment of all humanity. It is nobody's business to spend as much money on safeguarding future human health as is spent in finding newer and stronger pesticides. In the use of pesticides it may be justifiable to take some risks; but if man is to act responsibly for posterity, these must be *calculated* risks. Only a really disinterested research body can properly calculate the risks. Even if this country's record is reasonably good, its inhabitants are at hazard so long as food is imported. International research and control are the only ways of guaranteeing the safety of posterity from dangerous pesticides.

We have already seen that there are problems of social ethics involved in man's present use of raw materials and pesticides. An even greater problem is raised by man's waste of water, abuse of the soil, and deforestation of the earth. These three are interconnected. If the topsoil is spoilt, then the ground water level falls; for the earth can no longer contain the moisture. If trees are cut down, the topsoil is endangered, and rainfall is likely to decrease. If land is overdrained, or rivers straightened, again the ground water level is affected, and fertility is decreased.

Before man started cutting down the forests for his own use, the earth was densely covered with trees in very many areas. For example, almost all Spain was once a forest. Man has cut down trees partly because he needed wood and partly because he needed to till the soil. Gradually the trees have disappeared, and this process has been inevitable. But now much of Spain is infertile plain. What is alarming is the speed at which the remaining forests are now disappearing.

Two-fifths of the annual world requirements for timber are for the manufacture of paper and packaging. A single edition of the *New York Times* eats up 150 acres of forest land. The manufacture of paper increases annually. As yet only eighty-eight copies of newspapers are sold per thousand human beings; and there is great scope for more and better packaging. The British paper industry plans an annual four per cent growth. Meanwhile there is a growing demand for timber for housing, mines, and other uses. There is a certain amount of re-afforestation. Here in Great Britain the Forestry Commission is said to be the biggest landowner in the country. But in the world as a whole the forests are shrinking fast: in Canada and the United States, in South America and Africa and Europe. America is using twice as much wood each year as is provided by new growth. There is said to be a net annual deficit of one billion cubic metres of timber—consumption is two and a half billion but new growth only one and a half billion cubic metres.

The effect of deforestation is twofold. The climate tends to change. A good example of this is afforded by the area round Petra in South Jordan. As the biblical record shows, this used to be a well-wooded area with decent rainfall. Now it is a desert, and dry, with occasional tropical storms which endanger what topsoil remains. Trees with their complex roots keep it in place. They trap the ground water in the soil. They soak up in their leaves rainfall which in turn evaporates and promotes further precipitation. They act as windbreaks. Their leaves form rich and fertile humus. Without trees the land begins to dry up. To-day the waste surfaces of the earth are larger than its forests, and the imbalance annually increases. This state of affairs would be tolerable if it could be quickly put right. It cannot. Forests take decades to grow. Once the climate has changed, it is difficult to alter. When the ground water has sunk below a certain depth, it is difficult to grow trees in the soil. Present deforestation means future infertility. The satisfaction of our present needs for timber (and the consequent "rise in our standard of living") means that future generations will enjoy fewer natural amenities than we do.

It is not merely deforestation that is responsible for lack of water. It seems that waste gases released into the lower atmosphere are gradually producing a warmer climate, with consequently less water. But this is as nothing compared with man's prodigal waste of water. Instead of using six or seven gallons, urban consumption is nearly a hundred gallons per person per day. Nobody minds wasting water, nor do many people have scruples about poisoning natural water supplies with effluent from factories. The industrial use of water is even more "wasteful" than private use; and, as production goes up, so does our consumption of water.

In Europe agriculture needs to draw twice as much moisture from ground water as from rainfall. The rest of the rain runs away, or evaporates. (In urban areas, which are always increasing, very little sinks into the ground.) Three-quarters of the water used for drinking and other purposes is derived from ground supplies. And yet the ground water level is steadily sinking. We are living on a national (and international) water deficit. The draining of marshes (nature's reservoirs) has assisted the process, and the regulation and drainage of rivers has hastened it still more. (Since the Rhine was regulated, its surface level has fallen by one and a half inches a year, thus lowering the surrounding water table.) This lowered level results in lowered fertility. If we use up water in this generation, it seems that there will be less for future generations. This raises an acute problem in social ethics. Are we justified in lowering the world's resources of unpolluted water? Is it right that this generation should squander its water resources for its own use (agricultural, industrial, and personal), if this means that there will be less for posterity? Is it right, at a time when increasing urbanization threatens the British countryside, to ruin yet more places of natural beauty by flooding valleys to create new reservoirs? Perhaps a solution may eventually be found by desalinization on a gigantic scale. As yet the process is far too costly for large-scale use, and it is uncertain that the water shortage can ever be solved in this way—or solved in time. Time is running out. If the water table sinks too deep, the topsoil crumbles and blows away as dust.

Loss of humus is perhaps man's most serious capital loss of all. Growth and fertility depend on the health of the soil. The composition of humus (the topsoil with a depth of up to eight feet) almost defies analysis. It is gradually developed over centuries. It has been calculated that it takes between three and ten centuries to form a single inch of humus. Compounded of organic and inorganic matter, with traces of minerals and with millions of living bacteria, it is formed by the action of light and air and water and by the chemical interaction of its components. Humus is irreplaceable, or at any rate it takes centuries to replace. Yet man in his thoughtlessness, ignorance, and greed has destroyed and is destroying this precious inheritance. For example, it has been calculated that in the United States millions of tons of soil are either blown or washed away annually. Destruction of the humus can be caused by deforestation or by lack of water, and so the land deteriorates to steppe or desert; or the same result can be brought about by monoculture or by the injudicious use of artificial fertilizers. Although the soil of Great Britain is on the whole well looked after, it must be remembered that a high proportion of our foodstuffs is imported, and it may not be many years before the exporting countries have insufficient food to support their own populations. Once again we are posed with a problem in social ethics which is international in scope. Those well-wishers who advocate the growing of more food to feed the hungry millions seldom reflect that emergency measures to produce more food now may result in ruining the chances of growing in the future even as much as we now produce. What should we do? Take emergency steps now, and trust that God will provide for the future by enlightening men with some fresh means of growing food or even of producing food? I have never heard the choice even discussed, although it surely affects the whole future of mankind.

Of course, if the population of the world were to decrease, many of the problems raised in this chapter would be alleviated, if they did not absolutely disappear. The human race is increasing at about the rate of ninety a minute (or 37 million a year). It is nearly doubling itself every thirty-five years. This means that there needs to be a daily increase in the food-bearing areas of the world. In fact there is, for various reasons, a daily deficit. If the population of the world were to decrease, this deficit would be more tolerable. Questions of birth control are engaging the attention to-day both of secular authorities (to discover methods that are safe, cheap, efficacious, and foolproof) and also of religious authorities (to discover whether such methods are morally justifiable and permissible). Something will have to be done, or there will be standing room only! It is unlikely that there will be any *voluntary* decrease in the world's present population. The desires to procreate and to bear children are very deep and powerful instincts in men and women, and most people want to leave children behind them when they die. Even if the birthrate does sharply decrease in the areas of the present population explosion, it is probable that this will be offset to a certain extent by a further reduction in infant mortality, so that a larger percentage of infants will survive beyond the age of puberty and reproduce themselves.

It may be, however, that there will be an involuntary decrease in the world population in the next few centuries. It is a truism that we are passing through a period of unprecedented and revolutionary change for man in his environment. For all his adaptability, it is not certain whether *homo sapiens* will be able to adapt himself to novel conditions. For man has only a limited self-control. He is befouling the air with pollution, and the water with poisons. He is endangering his body and reproductive system by radioactivity. He is eating food which does not properly nourish him and additives which may injure him. He is consuming quantities of drugs the long term effects of which are unknown. He is subjecting himself to the dreadful strains of increasing speed and ceaseless, often severe, noise and vibration. His way of life is rapidly changing, and he is cutting himself off more and more from what is his natural environment. Indeed our countryside itself is beginning to disappear. He may welcome these changes with his conscious mind; but he has no control over his subconscious reactions. His diencephalon reacts to fear and other emotions in the same way as it did before *homo sapiens* evolved; and the results of this can be seen in increased nervous disorders and psychosomatic illnesses. It is the countries with the highest standard of living which tend to have the highest suicide rates. In the past many species of animals have disappeared because they could not adapt themselves to a changing environment. Possibly the same fate awaits man. But there is little enough that can be done about this. The forces of "progress" are irresistible. And, after all, the failure of man to adapt is highly problematical. At worst it is a risk; and the risk must be taken, for there is no alternative.

The problems raised in this chapter are real, but remote. They are forced on our attention by the present speed of change. They concern matters of *social* ethics; that is to say, any action taken by an individual is unlikely to be relevant to the problem or its solution. The dilemma facing us to-day can mostly be summed up in a single question: "To what extent is it morally right for man to use his dominion over nature without reference to posterity?" We must look far further ahead than the mere thirty years which was the limit of the British Association's prospect at its Cambridge Meeting in 1965. The answer that we give to our question will partly depend on how we distinguish between luxury and necessity; but the most important consideration concerns our view about the probable extent to which posterity will be able to look after itself.

If any action should be taken to curb man's exploitation of nature, it will be effective only if carried out and enforced internationally. It is a matter of MRI—mutual responsibility and interdependence. As yet, the scope of man's moral concern has not kept pace with the range of his exploitation over nature. Even over a small matter such as the production of whale oil (which threatens the extinction of a species) there is as yet no way to compel nations to honour an agreement which was made only with great difficulty. How much more difficult it would be to extend the scope of agreements to the exploitation of nature in general!

Long before agreements can be made, the problems must be publicly ventilated and properly studied. The object of this chapter is modest: simply to raise these uncomfortable issues, whether or not it is already too late to take effective remedial action.